The Gender Agenda

Agenda

Redefining Equality

by Dale O'Leary

Vital Issues Press

Vital Issues Press
P.O. Box 53788
Lafayette, Louisiana 70505

Library of Congress Card Catalog Number 96-60583
ISBN 1-56384-122-3

Printed in the U.S.A.

Dedication

To Mary and Alvaro
and
my wonderful husband,
without whose support
this book would not
have been possible.

Contents

Acknowledgments

My work on this book began with a series of articles published in *Catholic World Report* on the Cairo and Beijing conferences and a booklet entitled "Gender: The Deconstruction of Women," which was prepared for the delegates to the Beijing conference. I wish to thank Phil Lawler, editor of *Catholic World Report*, for permission to include the material from *Catholic World Report*, for his contributions to those articles, and for his support.

I also wish to thank all the members of the Coalition for Women and the Family who helped me with this project, especially Dan Zeidler and Christine and Alberto Vollmer. And, I wish to pay my respects to the courageous delegates who fought for women and the family.

I especially want to thank Genevieve Kineke and Abigail Tardiff, who helped me with the editing and gave me moral support, and all those who prayed for me and for this book.

Part I

One

Feminism and Gender

Without fanfare or debate, the word *gender* has been substituted for the word *sex*. We used to talk about sex discrimination, but now it's gender discrimination. Forms, like credit applications, used to ask for an indication of our sex, but now they ask for our gender. It certainly seems innocent enough. *Sex* has a secondary meaning—sexual intercourse or sexual activity. *Gender* sounds more delicate and refined. But, if you think the change signals a renaissance of neo-Victorian sensitivity, you could not be more wrong. This change, and a number of other things you may not have taken much notice of, are all part of the Gender Agenda.

Those who believed that the defeat of the Equal Rights Amendment signaled the end of the militant feminist era need to take another look. The militant feminists are back; they are ensconced in places of power and are determined to enforce a new version of their revolution—the Gender Agenda. Those who think affirmative action is an idea whose time has passed may be very surprised to find that there is an active movement to enforce worldwide fifty/fifty-male/female quotas.

The militant feminists have learned from their defeats. When they couldn't sell their radical ideology to ordinary women, they repackaged it. Now, they are very careful not to reveal their actual goals. They have worked themselves into positions of power within existing institutions. They intend to achieve their ends not by open confrontation, but by changing the meanings of words. The wrapping may be different, but the contents are just as unacceptable.

Listening to Feminists

My interest in feminism began with the publication of Betty Friedan's *Feminine Mystique*. The book came out right after I graduated from Smith College, which also happened to be Ms. Friedan's alma mater. My fellow alumnae were excited about Ms. Friedan's "myth-shattering" insights, but I found myself unconvinced. As the years passed, the more I heard about feminism, the less I liked it. Feminists claimed to promote the progress of women, but the feminists appeared to me to have a very warped idea of what it meant to be a woman, and an even weirder idea of what constitutes progress.

Intrigued by what appeared to me to be obvious contradictions in the feminist ideology, I decided to investigate feminism. I read the popular feminist writers: Simone de Beauvoir, Betty Friedan, Kate Millett, Susan Brownmiller, Gloria Steinem, and numerous others. Oppression of women certainly does not seem to have prevented them from getting books published. Libraries and bookstores display stacks of feminist literature. The *New York Times* book review section regularly publishes glowing reviews of the latest weighty feminist tomes.

Most of the books I read had a common theme: Men are monsters, and women always and everywhere have been oppressed. The weight of this evidence might have been convincing (certainly many others had been converted by it to the feminist cause); however, I wasn't convinced because what they said was contrary to my experience.

For example, feminists talked about how all women in the 1950s had been oppressed, but I had lived in the 1950s and knew firsthand that the things they said weren't true for all women. Feminists talked about the oppression of women in the nineteenth century, but my grandmother and great aunts had grown up in the nineteenth century and they weren't oppressed. They were tough, resilient women. My mother's mother supported the family when her husband lost his job and his confidence. My father's mother managed to hold the family together when her husband went blind. My great aunts were professional women. After several months of reading feminist diatribes, I said to my husband, "I don't understand why feminists are always complaining about oppression. I have never been oppressed." He smiled and replied, "Of course you haven't. No one would ever dare."

Indeed, no one had ever dared, or if they had, I hadn't noticed. My doting father encouraged me to major in physics. My mother wanted me to be a lawyer. One of my grandfathers taught me Greek; the other, Shakespeare, art, and poetry. My teachers supported my aspirations. No one ever told me that girls weren't as intelligent as boys, and if they had, I wouldn't have believed them. In my high school, girls played sports, participated in all activities, and equaled boys in academic subjects and standardized test scores. My mother was the vice-president of a small company. My grandmother was born in 1884 and had a woman doctor who was older than she was. My mother had a woman obstetrician when I was born. My husband and I had a woman doctor. Lest anyone think that I lived a privileged life or was part of an idealistic leftist community, let me assure you that I grew up in an ordinary family in small town America.

While I was not naive enough to believe that my positive experiences were universal, I could not suppress the suspicion that the feminist writers were prone to universalizing their own negative experiences.

Understanding the Pain

I am skeptical about one-size-fits-all historical theory, and particularly skeptical about conspiracy theories of history. Furthermore, I find the feminist theory of the universal oppression of women insulting. I simply refuse to believe that all my foremothers and all the women of the world had been so stupid that they had allowed themselves to be enslaved and abused, or that all the men in the world were so smart that they had been able to create this massive conspiracy. I know too many smart women.

History, it is true, is full of stories of the abuse of women, denials of women's rights, and violence against women, but it is also full of abuse, violence, and denials of human rights in general. Men, women, and children have been victims in every age. Every time a woman was abused it wasn't necessarily because she was a woman.

No one can deny that women have suffered, but outrage at the abuse of women doesn't solve the problem. Agreeing with the feminists that women have suffered does not require agreeing that the feminists have the solution to end that suffering. The feminists offer radical revolutionary solutions when far simpler changes would suffice. A woman who goes to the doctor with an infected toe is looking for a simple solution, not to have her foot amputated. It is true that a guillotine will solve the problem of migraine headaches, but most people would not consider it a viable solution.

Reading the feminist accounts of the emotional, physical, and sexual abuse of women, one senses that the feminists identify with the suffering of women because they themselves have suffered. One must ask, however, if it is suffering that makes a woman a feminist, or the inability to deal with suffering. Many women have had difficult lives and suffered terrible abuse, yet have been able to forgive and get on with their lives. They learned how to turn adversity into triumph.

The feminists I read obsessed over negative comments which other women would have laughed off. They seemed unable to distinguish male humor from male abuse. They couldn't forget the slightest insult, and they absolutely, positively would not forgive.

As I read through the feminist texts, I was reminded of the prayer "God grant me the serenity to accept the things I cannot change, the courage to change the things I can and the wisdom to know the difference." To me, it appeared that the feminists lack that crucial wisdom. They rage at things that can't be changed—like human nature—and accept things which can be changed—like their attitude toward past offenses.

In all this I could see nothing that was liberating for women, and much that would psychologically handicap women. I would have willingly joined them in a battle to eliminate real abuses and make life better for ordinary women, but the militant feminists' idea of positive change was pulling down the family, promoting sexual liberation, and defending abortion on demand.

Ideologies should be judged objectively, but in studying feminism and the Gender Agenda, it is difficult to put aside the suspicion that the entire enterprise is a giant rationalization created by hurt women to justify their anger, grudges, and self-destructive behavior. Their abortions, sexual promiscuity, rejection of motherhood, and lesbianism seem more like the acting out that results from childhood trauma than courageous self-liberation. Sometimes it is easier to blame oppressive structures and demand that the world change, than to admit responsibility for one's own self-destructive behavior.

Gloria's Story

Gloria Steinem, the darling of the feminist movement and editor of *Ms.* magazine, exemplifies the relationship between personal experience and feminist activism. To the world, Steinem presents herself as the epitome of the liberated woman, but in her book, *Outrageous Acts and Everyday Rebellions*, she reveals that behind the cosmopolitan image is a little girl who was afraid she would grow up to be like her mentally ill mother.

Steinem's mother was diagnosed with anxiety neurosis and required periodic institutionalization and medication. Steinem's father deserted the family, leaving teen-age Gloria to cope with a "crazy mother" who was afraid to leave the house and would lie in bed talking to herself. Gloria tried to take care of her mother as well as she could, but admits that she was obsessed with the fear that she would end up like her mother:

> Many years passed before I saw my mother as a person and before I understood that many of the forces in her life are patterns women share. Like a lot of daughters, I suppose I couldn't afford to admit that what had happened to my mother was not all personal or accidental and therefore could happen to me. [Gloria Steinem, *Outrageous Acts and Everyday Rebellions* (New York: Holt, Rinehart and Winston, 1983), p. 144]

As her mother benefited from treatment and was able to emerge from her withdrawal, Gloria struggled to understand the woman her mother had been before her illness:

> I used to say, "But why didn't you leave? Why didn't you take the job? Why didn't you marry the other man?" She would always insist it didn't matter, she was lucky to have my sister and me. If I pressed hard enough, she would add, "If I'd left you never would have been born."

> I always thought but never had the courage to say: *But you might have been born instead.* [Steinem, p. 139]

Reading the story of Gloria's youth, one cannot help but have compassion for the young girl left alone to cope with a "crazy mother." One can see how Gloria could blame herself for her mother's illness—if only she hadn't been born, her mother might have escaped from the marriage that Gloria sees as the cause of her mother's mental breakdown. Years later when asked about her mother she would say, "My mother was not mentally ill. She was defeated by a biased world" [Marcia Cohen, *The Sisterhood* (New York: Simon & Schuster, 1988), p. 50].

In 1956 Gloria found herself pregnant by a young man who wanted to marry her. She was able to arrange an abortion in England. When asked years later what would have happened if she had the baby, she replied:

> I don't know what I would have done. I really don't know . . . If I had to come home and got married and had a child . . . Maybe I would be functioning . . . Maybe I would have survived, but I don't see myself surviving . . . not in any real way. . . .

> I can only imagine going quietly crazy . . . [Cohen, p. 106]

One can understand why Gloria believes that marriage and children can drive a woman crazy and why she cannot admit that her mother's condition could have been the manifestation of a mental illness that could have occurred even if her mother had a perfect husband or had never married and had children.

I can feel compassion for the real suffering which Steinem and other feminists have undoubtedly experienced, but that does not force me to accept their theories or their schemes. Feminists can't be allowed to tear down all families and destroy all marriages because they are afraid of marriage and mother-hood.

Not all those attracted to feminism have had difficult child-hoods. Sometimes, the feminists reminded me of little girls standing beneath a boys' tree hut. Forbidden to enter because they were girls, some of them vowed in their childish hearts that one day they would force their way into that tree hut. Others vowed that when they grew up they would cut down the tree; if they couldn't play, no one could. Still others became determined that they would never again allow anyone to call them girls. I have to admit that I had been spared this envy because when I was young, I had talked my way into the boys' tree hut and discovered that nothing all that exciting was happening there.

Unbalanced Histories

Reading through feminist texts, it is easy to feel outraged at the catalogue of abuses, but anyone with a knowledge of history can recognize that these litanies of abuse are only one side of the story. For every victim the feminists mention, there is a heroine they ignore, or worse, turn into a victim. For example, feminists routinely complain about how the patriar-chal Puritans suppressed women, yet the feminists themselves neglect to mention the heroic Puritan women who were fa-mous in their day, such as Anne Bradstreet, who was the first published American poet, male or female.

In her book on rape, Susan Brownmiller fails to credit the courage of Goodwife Mary Rowlandson, whose account of her captivity during the King Philip War in 1676 was the first American best seller. Worse still, Brownmiller implies that Rowlandson might have been lying when she insisted that the Indians who held her captive had not "offered the least abuse of unchastity to me in word or action" [Susan Brownmiller, *Against Our Will* (New York: Bantam, 1976), p. 151].

The feminist writers talked of the importance of positive role models for women; I agree. But, it is they who have demeaned, ignored, or distorted the stories of strong confident women like Catherine Beecher, a nineteenth-century advocate for women; Frances Willard, a Christian activist who masterminded the Women's Temperance Union and was key to women winning the right to vote; Sarah Pierpoint Edwards, a mystic considered by her contemporaries as having more spiritual insight than her husband Jonathan Edwards; Susanna Wesley, the mother of nineteen, including John and Charles Wesley, the founders of the Methodist church who gave her all the credit for their work; St. Catherine of Sienna, named a doctor of the Catholic church for her mystical theology, from whom the pope took advice.

Feminist theologians insist that the Bible suppressed the stories of women, but one can easily find many heroic women in Scripture, including Jael, who killed the enemy of her people by driving a tent peg through his temple, and Judith, who chopped off the head of Holofernes with two whacks of his own sword, and thus rated her own book in the Bible.

I found so many factual errors and distortions in feminist writings that I could have spent a lifetime providing the documentation to correct them. For example, Susan Brownmiller sees patriarchal oppression in the fact that "Judith and her Book appear in the nether regions of the dubious Apocrypha" [Brownmiller, p. 365]. Contrary to Brownmiller's assertion that Judith "was not the sort of role model that any patriarchy in its right mind would wish to put forward" [Brownmiller, p. 365], the Book of Judith is included in all Catholic Bibles. At the time of the Reformation, for reasons which had nothing to do with Judith's threat to "patriarchal" ideology, the Lutherans relegated all parts of the Old Testament which were written in Greek to "Apocrypha" status. This included the Book of Judith. Furthermore, Judith's story was a favored subject in Catholic art. On the ceiling of the Sistine Chapel, the room where the pope's election takes place, Michaelangelo depicted Judith deftly making off with Holofernes' head. The fresco of Judith is balanced by one of David cutting off the head of Goliath, demonstrating both symbolic symmetry and sexual equality. And, Judith is not the only woman on the ceiling. Female sibyls are balanced with male prophets, while the male and female ancestors of Jesus are shown without discrimination.

The more I read, the more errors I found. If everything I was familiar with was incorrect, I could only assume that those things with which I was unfamiliar were probably equally flawed.

History is not the only thing distorted by feminist writers. Christina Hoff Sommers, in her book, *Who Stole Feminism?*, documents how the feminists have created myths about violence against women, distorted research on teen-age girls' self-esteem, and suppressed evidence which didn't fit their theories. The feminists have railed against the suppression of women by men, and then turned around and suppressed any woman who opposed their ideology. Women researchers who study the differences between men and women are often denied funding and routinely warned to choose a different line of inquiry. Gloria Steinem decries such research as antiwoman: "It's really the remnant of anti-American, crazy thinking, to do this kind of research. It's what's keeping us down, not what's helping us" [John Stossel, "Boys and Girls are Different: Men, Women, and the Sex Difference," ABC News Special, 1 February 1995].

Lastly, while feminists have been known to state plainly that they consider logic "a patriarchal plot," I believe that the various arguments an author presents should not be contradictory. The feminists had only one point: "men are awful"—and everything was viewed as proof. If men raped women, that was oppression—agreed. But, if men were outraged at rape, that, according to the feminists, was also evidence of oppression. Slamming a door in women's faces was oppression, but opening the door was also oppressive. Marrying women and condemning them to family life was oppressive, but so was not marrying them. Men were damned if they did and damned if they didn't.

Feminist evidence was unconvincing, their theories contradictory, and besides this, something about feminism sounded vaguely and unpleasantly familiar. I had heard this tune before, but I couldn't quite remember the words. Eventually, I discov-

ered there was a great deal more wrong with feminism than I
had imagined. As I probed further, the music became louder
and clearer, and ultimately I discovered whose song they were
singing.

Cairo to Beijing

Feminism is only one of many issues that divides the parties in the culture wars. Since I had been tracking, reporting,
and commenting on the various battles in this conflict for over
fifteen years, it was not surprising that in 1994 I was interested
in the preparations for the U.N. Conference on Population in
Cairo. The battle over Cairo had been heating up for months.
Eight weeks before the conference began, the opportunity to
cover the Cairo conference presented itself, and I jumped at the
chance. Population issues are not my area of expertise, but it
appeared clear by mid-July that the conflict in Cairo was crucial, and anyone who wanted to be where the action was had
better be there.

In the culture wars, the location may change, but the issues
remain the same. The sex and life issues dominated the debates
in Cairo just as they do at local school board meetings, outside
abortion clinics, and in the halls of Congress. For me, the road
from Cairo led to Beijing and the U.N. Fourth World Conference on Women.

What happened in Cairo and Beijing matters. Not so much
because the U.N. can force its will on the United States, for
only poor countries who depend on foreign aid will be forced
to accept the agendas promulgated at these conferences. It
matters because the culture war is a battle of ideas, and the
U.N. has the resources and prestige to promote its agenda to
world leaders, schoolchildren, and the media.

At the moment, the U.N. is devoting its resources and
prestige to promoting the "gender perspective," and the supporters of this Gender Agenda expect more than talk. They
have demanded that the plans made in Cairo and in Beijing be
implemented and funded. The Platform for Action of the
Beijing conference on women called on governments to "main-

stream a gender perspective" in every program and policy in every public and private institution.

The Clinton administration, the Canadian government, the European Union, and a host of U.N. agencies are busily "mainstreaming the gender perspective," but there has been very little discussion in the media about exactly what a "gender perspective" entails. If a "gender perspective" is about to be "mainstreamed" in every public and private program in the world, prudence would require that, at the very least, the public be informed as to the nature of this agenda. Instead, implementation proceeds without public enlightenment. The Gender Agenda sails into communities not as a tall ship, but as a submarine, determined to reveal as little of itself as possible.

Those who are willing to search through U.N. documents can, however, find a definition of the gender perspective and its goals. According to a booklet published by the United Nations International Research and Training Institute for the Advancement of Women (INSTRAW), "To adopt a gender perspective is '... *to distinguish between what is natural and biological and what is socially and culturally constructed, and in the process to renegotiate the boundaries between the natural—and hence relatively inflexible—and the social—and hence* relatively *transformable*' " ["Gender Concepts in Development Planning: Basic Approach" (INSTRAW, 1995), p. 11]. In plain English, it means that the evident differences between men and women aren't natural, but were made up, and can and should be changed.

Is this gender perspective a self-evident truth which should, without debate or discussion, be imposed upon all the peoples of the world? What is the relationship between the gender perspective and the fact that its proponents have an extreme aversion to words like *mother*, *father*, *husband*, and *wife*? Why do the advocates of the Gender Agenda refer to marriage and family in negative terms? Why does a U.N. document about women have almost nothing positive to say about women who are full-time mothers? Why does the U.N. no longer promote a "woman's perspective"?

The forces behind the U.N. Fourth World Conference on Women believe that their "gender perspective" is a self-evident truth. They were busy even before the Beijing conference putting in place their plans to "mainstream the gender perspective" in every school, every business, every family, every public and private program, at every level, and in every country. Given the power of the forces behind it, the speed at which it is being implemented, and what is at stake, the Gender Agenda demands, at the very least, strict scrutiny.

Naming the Participants

Chronicling an ideological conflict requires naming the participants. You can't speak of how "they" did this and how "they" did that without defining who "they" are. Since this conflict involves two large and diverse coalitions held together only by a general commitment to certain principles, listing the members of the coalition would be awkward, if not impossible. The leaders of the coalition of groups promoting the Gender Agenda call themselves feminists, but advocacy of the Gender Agenda is not limited to women nor to those whose major concern is feminism. Support for the Gender Agenda comes from activist groups, all somewhat interrelated or overlapping in interest, but nevertheless distinguishable: 1) population controllers; 2) sexual libertarians; 3) gay rights activists; 4) multiculturalists/promoters of political correctness; 5) environmental extremists; 6) neo-Marxists/progressives; 7) postmodernists/ deconstructionists. The Gender Agenda is also supported by big-government liberals and certain multinational corporations.

The term *gender feminists* seems most appropriate for a coalition of interest groups promoting the Gender Agenda, since they have taken as their goal "mainstreaming the gender perspective" in every program and policy in the public and private sector. It seems fair to say that they are interested in establishing gender as the governing force of the world. At times, it would be more accurate to speak of the Gender Establishment, since the promotion of the gender perspective is not being accomplished by grassroots activists, or ordinary women, but by people who have established themselves within various centers of power and are using their influence to forward this agenda.

Politeness generally requires calling people by the name they have chosen for themselves. In the case of feminists, however, this presents difficulties, since women with radically different philosophies call themselves feminists. Gender feminists do not refer to themselves by that name. Instead, they call themselves feminists and pretend to represent all women. Besides this, there are other forms of feminism which preceded gender feminism and which continue to have an influence.

In 1977, in a textbook designed for women's studies programs, Alison Jagger identified liberal, Marxist, socialist, radical, lesbian, and matriarchal separatist forms of feminism [Alison Jagger, "Political Philosophies of Women's Liberation," *Feminism and Philosophy* (Totowa, NJ: Littlefield, Adams & Co., 1977) p. 5-37]. Christina Hoff Sommers distinguishes between old, mainstream, or equity feminism (roughly equivalent to liberal feminism) and new, "resenter" (angry at men), or gender feminism. Recently, some have taken to distinguishing between liberal, radical, Marxist, and postmodernist feminists.

Some have suggested that the term *feminist* should be reserved for liberal feminists and others referred to as "feminist extremists." This would give the inaccurate impression that the "feminist extremists" are atypical, which is not the case. Liberal feminists are not the dominant force in the women's movement. Among feminist theorists and feminist activists, the percentage of liberal feminists grows smaller every year. Furthermore, women who even suggest moderation are often castigated by "true believers" as traitors to the cause or captives of "backlash."

A number of women have chosen to call themselves pro-life feminists or Christian feminists. They feel that the word is broad enough to include all women who believe in women's rights and women's equality. While the desire to express support for women is understandable, it seems to me that there is a substantial difference between being for women and being for feminism. Whatever positive image the word *feminist* may have had, it has been tarnished by those who have made it their own, and I, for one, am content to leave the militants in full possession of the term. But, that leaves us with the problem of what to call those who oppose militant feminism.

While many Americans are politically dyslexic, the terms *Left* and *Right* are still useful. In the culture wars, the Left generally supports sexual liberation, sexually explicit entertainment, abortion on demand, homosexual rights, contraceptive-based sex education, quotas, and affirmative action, while the Right supports marriage, the family, life, chastity, and equality of opportunity.

The feminists label their opponents "fundamentalists," "the Religious Right," or "right-wing extremists," implying that they represent a narrow, extremist, sectarian religious point of view which has no place in the public arena. The opponents of the Gender Agenda are, however, united not by adherence to a particular religion, but by a commitment to the family and a belief in human nature. They think of themselves as profamily.

Feminists insist that they too support the family, but they redefine family so that the term could refer to two roommates and their dog. On the other hand, most profamily activists would support the following definition of the family:

> The "family" in all ages and in all corners of the globe can be defined as a man and a woman bonded together through a socially approved covenant of marriage to regulate sexuality, to bear, raise, and protect children, to provide mutual care and protection, to create a small home economy, and to maintain continuity between the generations, those going before and those coming after. It is out of the reciprocal, naturally recreated relations of the family that broader communities—such as tribes, villages, peoples, and nations—grow. [Allan Carlson, "What's Wrong With the United Nations' Definition of 'Family'?" *The Family in America* (August 1994), p.3]

Profamily advocates are unequivocal in their support for women's equal rights. They believe that all men are created equal and endowed by their Creator with certain inalienable rights; they have no doubt that "all men" refers to men and women equally.

Profamily advocates have been falsely accused of hating people who do not agree with them, women who have abortions, and men and women who engage in homosexual acts and other forms of self-destructive behavior. In fact, profamily people care deeply about these people as individuals and worry about their health and welfare, but they also worry about society and innocent people who will be harmed if dangerous policies are promoted.

Many women believe that feminism is so destructive and contrary to the best interests of women, that they actively oppose feminism. Women who are prowoman and antifeminism believe just as passionately in women's equality. These women never doubted they were equal as persons to men, although some would agree with my mother, who loved to say that she didn't want equality with men since she had no intention of stepping down. These women don't want inclusive language. They consider themselves included in the word *man*. They prefer *chairman* to *chair*, *wife* to *spouse*, and *Mrs.* or *Miss* to *Ms.* They call God *Father*, and believe that *sons of God* refers to them as much as to their brothers.

To be prowoman and antifeminism is not to ignore the problems women face in their everyday lives, and certainly not to excuse abuse, violence, exploitation, or unjust discrimination against women or anyone else, but to believe that a feminist revolution not only won't solve the problems of ordinary women, it will make things worse.

The U.N.

Some people have asked why I have bothered to write a book about the United Nations. Isn't the U.N. irrelevant? To this I respond: This isn't a book about the U.N.; it is a book about the Gender Agenda, the redefinition of equality, and the war on motherhood. I could have written about how the Gender Agenda is being promoted in the universities, in public schools, in government, in the media, or even in business, but the U.N. Conference on women was a unique opportunity to see the entire Gender Agenda laid out in one place.

Because the Gender Establishment firmly controls the U.N., they have been open about revealing the full scope of their plans to remake the world. It was easy to get it all in writing in their own words. Because in public debates the defenders of the Gender Agenda are less than forthcoming about their intentions, I have included a large number of quotations.

Some may think that this book backs up the contention that the U.N. should be abolished or at least kicked out of the U.S. While I can understand that sentiment, my personal experiences in Cairo and Beijing made me realize that the U.N. has much to offer as a place where the people of the world can meet and learn to understand one another. We do have a duty to be concerned about the needs of others and how our policies affect those in other countries. Unfortunately, the U.N. has become captive to dangerous ideologues, who are using the U.N.'s power and influence to forward their dangerous schemes.

The U.N. should not try to become an international government, or worse, an international bureaucracy, but a place for sovereign nations to meet, where the voices of the small, the poor, and the powerless can be heard. Pope John Paul II in his speech to the U.N. in October 1995 chose to speak about the rights of nations, respect for differences, and the fundamental right to freedom of religion and freedom of conscience. These are clearly threatened by some who wish to use the U.N. to impose an ideological straitjacket on the world.

What happened in Beijing does matter, because what was planned in Beijing will be coming to every town, every school, and every business (if it isn't there already)—unless it is exposed and we stand up against it.

Two

Mainstreaming the Gender Perspective

A few months after I returned from the Beijing conference, a woman approached me at a social gathering. "I heard you were in Beijing. Tell me about it," she said. "It must have been exciting. I read all about it." As I explained a little about what had gone on, she was shocked. "I never heard any of this in the press." She was correct. While U.N. conferences attract substantial media attention, the mainstream media seemed determined to avoid the real story and focus on peripheral issues.

The Beijing conference on women was no exception. The coverage concentrated on China's human rights violations, Hillary Clinton's attendance, Chinese harassment of women attending the associated Non-Governmental Organizations Forum—but not on the central theme of the conference— "mainstreaming a gender perspective." With affirmative action and quotas a hot issue at home, one would think that the reporters might point out that the platform calls for across-the-board quotas. With family values a major political football, it might be expected that the press would note the negative treatment of marriage, family, and motherhood in the text.

But, this failure on the part of the media is hardly surprising, since they have consistently failed to investigate the Gender Agenda and the ideological implications behind it, even though the Gender Agenda is everywhere, as the following examples demonstrate. These examples have been paired with applicable paragraphs from the Beijing platform.*

♦   ♦   ♦   ♦   ♦

Forced Equality

Brown University in Providence, Rhode Island, a member of the prestigious Ivy League and recognized as a leader in its commitment to women's equality, diversity, and multiculturalism, was recently sued for discrimination against women. Brown was charged with violating Title IX, which mandates that educational institutions which received government funds must provide equal opportunities for participation in sports to women and men. Brown had willingly increased the number of teams for women, providing more women team sports than any other college. When a budget crunch came, Brown cut women's and men's teams equally, but the women's coaches took Brown to court, arguing that while the student body at Brown is more than 50 percent female, participation in interscholastic sports is 60 percent male/40 percent female.

The university presented evidence that male students are more interested in playing sports than female students; that more men go out for sports in high school and in college than women; that men are willing to sit on the bench and never play a single game, whereas women who feel they will never play frequently quit the team. The school argued that the existing women's teams had vacant slots and, therefore, ample opportunity already existed for women who wished to participate in a team sport at Brown.

---

* The number and/or letter preceding the quotations from the Beijing Declaration and Platform for Action references the paragraph from which the excerpt was taken. Some of the quotations are preceded by two numbers. This is necessary because the first number is from the draft and is the number which was used during the discussions. The second number in brackets is the one used in the final document where some of the numbering was changed because of additions and subtractions. The same system of referencing the document will be used through this book for the sake of clarity.

The judge ruled that if Brown could not raise the number of women, they would have to lower the number of men, until statistically equal participation between men and women was achieved.

> Beijing Platform 280(d)—Promote the full and equal participation of girls in extracurricular activities, such as sports, drama and cultural activities.

Gender Enforcement

In the wake of the Brown case, the U.S. Department of Education published new rules requiring colleges and universities to issue yearly reports on how much they spend for men's and women's intercollegiate athletics. Advocates for female athletes said the new rules could make it easier for them to prove charges of sexual discrimination ["Colleges Told to Publish Sports Costs," *New York Times* (3 December 1995)].

> Beijing Platform 209(a)—Ensure that statistics related to individuals are collected, compiled, analyzed and presented by sex and age and reflect problems, issues and questions related to women and men in society.

Coed Basketball

In an article in the Education section of the *New York Times*, Dr. Charles Corbin, professor of health and physical education at Arizona State University at Tempe was quoted as saying: "If boys and girls are equally matched by age, ability, experience, height and weight, girls can play on boys' teams and vice versa . . . It's more enjoyable, fun, and real life."

Dr. William Squires, professor of biology, health fitness, and nutrition at Texas Lutheran College stated, "If you had an informed society, you could have a coed basketball league and have the three best boys and three best girls on one team play another school's three best boys and three best girls."

On the other hand, Mary E. Dunquin, professor of sports psychology/sociology at the University of Pittsburgh thinks the answer is no contact sports at all [Elaine Louie, "Unequal Contest," *New York Times*: Education (July 1989), p. 29].

In North Kingston, Rhode Island, the junior high school gym classes are coed. Boys and girls wrestle each other. Some of the boys are so embarrassed they have refused to take part, while others have embraced the situation.

> Beijing Declaration 24—Take all necessary measures to eliminate all forms of discrimination against women and the girl child and remove all obstacles to gender equality.

Outrunning Men

According to an article in the *New York Times*, research done by Dr. Susan Ward and Dr. Brian Whipp, physiologists at UCLA, suggest that

> if women's running performance continues to improve at the rate at which it has soared since the 1920's, the top women will soon be running as swiftly as the best men, and may even outrun them someday. . . . The researchers suggest that elite female runners have been getting so much faster at such a rapid pace that they should be running marathons as quickly as men by 1998 and other shorter track events before the middle of the next century.
>
> These startling predictions are based on a new statistical analysis that compares trends in men's and women's world records over the past 70 years and projects those patterns into the future.

The researchers admit that the fleetest female runners today would not even qualify for the men's track events in the Olympics—the men's world record (for the marathon) is 2:06.50, the woman's 2:21.06, but they are sure that the differences can be overcome. [Natalie Angier, "2 Experts Say Women Who Run May Overtake Men," *New York Times* (7 January 1992), p. c3]

> Beijing Platform 28 [27]—In many countries, the differences between women's and men's achievements and activities are still not recognized as the consequences of socially constructed gender roles rather than immutable biological differences.

Female Football Coaches

The Department of Education in the state of Rhode Island, in conjunction with the Commission on Women, is promoting gender equity programs in every public and private school in the state. The program was initiated after a survey revealed inequalities in education in Rhode Island, including the fact that 100 percent of the football coaches are men. The report admits that in coaching, "no women apply for vacancies and in many other instances the quality and years of experience place women at a distinct disadvantage when they do apply for positions. Recruitment efforts and support programs need to be provided to increase the number of women in coaching."

The report concluded: "Intervention to change attitudes toward gender stereotyped careers and to increase interest in nontraditional areas must begin in kindergarten and continue throughout school" [Kathryn Quina, "Report Card for the 1990's: A Report on the Status of Girls and Women in Rhode Island Education" (Rhode Island Commission on Women, July 1992)].

> Beijing Platform 85(m) [83]—Support the advancement of women in all areas of athletics and physical activity including coaching.

Stepsiblings and Child Scouts

U.S. Supreme Court Justice Ruth Bader Ginsburg's work on a study of sex bias in the U.S. legal code secured her reputation as a champion of women's rights. Ginsburg, who was at the time professor of law at Columbia Law School, and Brenda Feigen-Fasteau, former director of the American Civil Liberties Union's Women's Rights Project, were commissioned to design a plan to erase "sex bias from our most basic laws." Their report, published in 1977, found numerous examples of sex bias.

It appears that they discovered that the U.S. code contained a number of laws which referred to "husbands and wives," rather than "spouses"; "fathers and mothers" rather than "parents"; "grandfathers and grandmothers" rather than "grandpar-

ents"; "sisters and brothers" rather than "siblings"; and "step-
sisters and stepbrothers" rather than "stepsiblings."

The report also expressed concern that the antilitter sym-
bol Johnny Horizon was a "sex stereotype of the outdoorsperson"
and "should be supplemented with a female figure promoting
the same values." Furthermore, "the two figures should be
depicted as persons of equal strength of character" [Ruth Bader
Ginsburg and Brenda Feigen-Fasteau, "Sex Bias in the US
Code" (*Report of the U.S. Commission on Civil Rights*, April
1977), p. 100].

The report criticized section 371 of the U.S. code which
deals with the validity of marriages contracted according to
Indian customs, because

> [t]he section contains unnecessary references to the sexes
> of the parties to the marriage. More substantively, it
> specifies that children of such unions shall be deemed to
> be the legitimate issue of the father, but makes no such
> specification as to the mother. Apparently, it was re-
> garded as beyond question that such children are the
> legitimate issue of the mother. The unique physical
> characteristic that the natural mother of a child is invari-
> ably present at the child's birth does not justify this
> distinction in all cases. [Ginsburg and Feigen-Fasteau,
> p. 119]

The report also complained about government support for
the Boy Scouts and Girl Scouts: "The Boy Scouts and Girl
Scouts, while ostensibly providing 'separate but equal' benefits
to both sexes perpetuate stereotyped sex roles" [Ginsburg and
Feigen-Fasteau, p. 145].

The report did support allowing the continued use of gender specific place names, such as Twin Sisters Mountain and
Minute Man National Park [p. 208].

> Beijing Platform 232(d)—Review national laws, includ-
> ing customary laws and legal practices in the areas of
> family, civil, penal, labour and commercial law
> and . . . revoke any remaining laws that discriminate on
> the basis of sex and remove gender bias in the admin-
> istration of justice.

Fifty/fifty Quotas for Congress

Mim Kelber, who was deeply involved in preparations for Non-Governmental Organization's (NGOs) participation in the Beijing conference, is the editor of the book *Women and Government: New Ways to Political Power*. Former Congresswoman Bella Abzug coauthored the introduction. The book, written explicitly for the Beijing conference, lays out plans for achieving fifty/fifty quotas in all elected offices. In the U.S. this would be achieved by, among other things, rewriting the Constitution to mandate that the Senate be composed of two hundred members, two women and two men from every state [Mim Kelber, *Women and Government: New Ways to Political Power* (Westport, CT: Praeger, 1994), pp. 215-218].

> Beijing Platform 192(a) [190]—[E]stablishing the goal of gender balance in governmental bodies and committees, as well as in public administrative entities, and in the judiciary, including, inter alia, setting specific targets and implementing measures to substantially increase the number of women with a view to achieving equal representation of women and men, if necessary through positive action, in all governmental and public administration positions; Take measures, including where appropriate, in electoral systems that encourage political parties to integrate women in elective and non-elective public positions in the same proportion and levels as men.

Lesbian Studies

Kathleen Westergaard, a student at the University of Victoria, British Columbia, Canada, received an assignment in her women's studies class. "Women in class will pair up and spend 10 minutes walking around campus holding hands. Feel free to be more demonstratively affectionate. Try to walk around crowded areas. When back in class you will report how it felt for you to do this. . . . If you are not able to make yourself do the exercise analyze why." Ms. Westergaard refused and filed a complaint. "I wanted a woman's studies degree because I believe in women's rights and fighting for equality. . . . They should change the name of the course to lesbian studies" [Steve Vanagas, "Lesbian conversion," *Western Report* (19 June 1995), p. 44].

According to University of Alberta anthropologist Ruth Gruhun, "The explicit objective of Women's Studies is political: the ideology is to be propagated as widely as possible, with the ultimate goal of achieving social change. . . . An ideology entrenched by formal institutionalization within the university, however, can be maintained far beyond its time, as long as it can be protected from criticism" [Steve Vanagas, "Lesbian conversion" *Western Report* (19 June 1950, p. 44].

> Beijing Platform 209(c) [206]—Involve centres for women's studies . . . in monitoring and evaluating the implementation of the goals of the Platform for Action.

Ask the Baby

Elias Farajojé-Jones, a divinity professor at Howard University, believes: "We are taught we have to be one thing. Now people are finding they don't have to choose." Farajojé-Jones, who has been sleeping with men and women since he was sixteen, has a two-month-old baby with his bisexual partner, Katherin. He has decided "that his child Issa-Ajamu will know no gender barriers. With help from a fillable, strap-on tube, both parents will breast-feed. And, when people ask if the child—who has both ears pierced—is a boy or a girl, Farajojé-Jones responds: 'Ask the baby' " [Steve Rhodes et al., "Bisexuality," *Newsweek* (17 July 1995), p. 49].

> Beijing Platform 245(a)—Promote the equal sharing of family responsibilities through media campaigns that emphasize gender equality and non-stereotyped gender roles of women and men within the family.

Ask the Transsexual

In San Francisco, the police are forced to deal with alleged perpetrators whose "chosen" sexual identity does not match their biological identity. To accommodate "transgendered" people, "unisex" bathrooms in addition to separate male and female bathrooms were suggested, but not required by legislation passed recently in San Francisco. Cynthia Goldstein of the San Francisco Human Rights Commission said that the city is "looking at a tiered system of accommodation . . . Whenever nudity is involved, such as a community shower, your genitals should match the facilities." Police were instructed to house transgendered people "in jail cells appropriate to the person's gender identity." According to the article, police were told: "It is respectful to ask a person whose gender identity is in question which gender they prefer." The problem of women who object to having to share a ladies room or dressing rooms in clothing stores with men dressed up like women still must be addressed [*Lambda Report on Homosexuality Newsletter*].

> Beijing Platform 125(k) [124]—Adopt all appropriate measures, especially in the field of education, to modify the social and cultural patterns of conduct of men and women.

No Privacy

Wendy Shalit, a sophomore at Williams College, reports that at the beginning of each year, male and female students in each dormitory unit gather in their common room to vote on whether or not to have a coed bathroom. The vote always goes coed because freshmen are harangued into voting for it, because if they vote for gender privacy they are accused of not being "comfortable with their bodies."

Miss Shalit, who insists that she is comfortable with her body, would like to use the bathroom in privacy. "In the world of the coed bathroom, young women are free to perform strip teases and parade about in wet towels secure in the knowledge that their college administration will come down like a hammer on any young man found guilty of 'objectifying' them with the 'male gaze'."

Ms. Shalit sees the bathroom situation as an "allegory of the present intellectual atmosphere in our universities where everything is relative, nothing is 'essentially' different from anything else, there are no fixed meanings—and in the name of this very open-mindedness students are daily invited to accommodate the most monstrous propositions, philosophical no less than sexual" [Jeffrey Hart, "Sex Re-education at Williams," *Providence Journal* (28 November 1995), p. B7].

> Beijing Platform 283(a)—[T]ake measures to eliminate
> incidents of sexual harassment of girls in educational
> and other institutions.

Our Father/Mother in Heaven

In the Oxford University Press's new inclusive language version of the New Testament and Psalms, the phrase "Son of Man" is translated "Human One." The Lord's Prayer begins "Our Father-Mother in heaven." References to the kingdom of God are dropped because the word *kingdom* has a "blatantly androcentric and patriarchal character." In the scene where Jesus' worried parents find him in the temple, the text now reads, " 'Why were you searching for me? Did you not know I must be in the house of my Father-Mother?' But they did not understand what Jesus said to them."

References to the right hand of God are dropped out of deference to left-handed people. Darkness is no longer used as an image of evil for fear of offending blacks.

Some think that this translation has not gone far enough. The Postmodernist Bible, a collection of essays produced by the Bible and Culture Collective, complains that "nothing is said of a God the Mother or of God made Woman, or even of God as a couple or couples. . . . We need to be liberated from the oppression of racism, classism, and sexism, that is, from patriarchy," argues the Collective. "The attention paid to Jesus' death diverts attention from that oppression" [Anthony Lane, "Scripture Rescripted," *New Yorker* (23 December 1995), p. 100].

> Beijing Platform 276(d)—Take steps so that tradition
> and religion and their expressions are not a basis for
> discrimination against girls.

Equal Exploitation

Hooters Restaurant, which promotes itself by hiring very attractive young women as waitresses and clothing them in skimpy outfits, has recently been charged with discrimination against men. The Equal Employment Opportunity Commission complaint charged that the refusal to hire male waiters constituted discrimination against men, even though no male had applied for a job as a waiter at Hooters. The EEOC demanded that Hooters agree to establish strict quotas—roughly fifty/fifty—hiring of women *and* men ["Who gives a hoot?" *Providence Journal* (3 December 1995)].

> Beijing Platform 165 [163]—[R]ethinking employment policies is necessary in order to integrate the gender perspective and to draw attention to a wider range of opportunities as well as to address any negative gender implications of current patterns of work and employment.

Safe Sex Plastic (W)rap

Lani Ka'ahumanu is the coordinator of the Safer Sex Sluts, an HIV education group. The group "does fun and funny skits that show the awkwardness of safer sex but also eroticizes it," says Ka'ahumanu who often opens the skits with her "Safer Sex Plastic (W)rap" ["Facts," *Ms.* (July/August 1994), p. 45].

> Beijing Platform 99—HIV/AIDS and other sexually transmitted diseases . . . are having a devastating effect on women's health, particularly the health of adolescent girls and young women. They often do not have the power to insist on safe and responsible sex.

> Strategic objective C.3—Undertake gender-sensitive initiatives that address sexually transmitted diseases, HIV/AIDS, and sexual and reproductive health issues.

Inflatable Dolls

The Non-Government Organizations Forum held in conjunction with the Beijing conference on women scheduled workshops on lesbian flirting and "The Role of Inflatable Life-size Plastic Dolls and Dildos in Improving Health." While the lesbian flirting workshop was well attended, the organizers of the dolls and dildos workshop didn't show up, leaving the

attendees to discuss the question among themselves. While
several decided the whole thing was a joke, American health
writer Rebecca Chalker disagreed. She suggested that the plastic or rubber dolls could be made lifelike and penetrable. They
could be mechanical and made-to-order. Men could go to the
store, choose a doll, and pick a background tape with a woman's
voice to accompany intercourse [Jennifer Griffin, *Beijing Watch*
(11 September 1995), p. 3].

> Beijing Platform 27 [26]—Women, through non-gov-
> ernmental organizations, have participated in and strongly
> influenced community, national, regional and global fo-
> rums and international debates.

Bisexuals and Prostitutes

A story in the *Wall Street Journal*, entitled "Dating Game
Today Breaks Traditional Gender Rules" discussed the current
trend to bisexual dating on campus:

> Young women openly enter into intimate relationships
> with both genders that are more than just experiments.
> They resist being described as straight or gay—or even
> bisexual, which some think suggests promiscuity and
> one-night stands. Instead they use words like *fluid* and
> *omnisexual*. . . . Tolerance of same-sex dating among
> women often begins on college campuses, where gay
> relationships raise few eyebrows these days. At her 1993
> graduation from Macalester College in St. Paul, Minn.,
> Laura Bradley stood before parents, grandparents, the
> school's board of trustees and faculty and read a letter to
> her mother who had died of cancer two years earlier. In
> the essay, she thanked her lover, Marcy. The two women
> later kissed on stage after receiving their diplomas.
> [Wendy Bounds, "Dating Games Today Breaks Tradi-
> tional Gender Roles," *Wall Street Journal* (26 April 1995),
> p. B1]

One of the newspapers published for the Beijing conferences carried a story entitled "Prostitutes Demand Dignity and
Legal Rights." According to the article, "Prostitutes say that
they should have the same rights as other working women,

including retirement benefits. . . . 'Prostitutes are no different from any other working women. . . . We are just ordinary women,' said Mexican prostitute Claudia Commimore Arellano. 'Like all women too, we worry about how much is a taxi, how to impose safe sex and how to avoid assault' " [Natacha Henry, *Beijing Watch* (11 September 1995), p. 3].

> Beijing Platform 97 [95]—The human rights of women include their right to have control over and decide freely and responsibly on maters related to their sexuality including sexual and reproductive health, free of coercion, discrimination and violence.

◆　　　◆　　　◆　　　◆　　　◆

Reading through these examples of the Gender Agenda, one does not know whether to laugh or weep. When ordinary people are exposed to examples of the gender perspective, the question they ask is, why? Why are those who claim to be the spokesmen for women advocating such absurd policies?

The promoters of the Gender Agenda talk about oppression and liberation, but the tune I was hearing wasn't a free melody, but a totalitarian rhythm which demanded that everyone march to the same beat.

Three

Understanding the Process

During the last twenty years, international conferences have become a major part of the United Nations' activities. Nafis Sadik, secretary general of the Cairo conference on population, claims that conferences now occupy 70 percent of the U.N.'s work. Since 1974 the U.N. has sponsored four conferences on women—Mexico City, 1975, Copenhagen, 1980, Nairobi, 1985, and Beijing, 1995; three conferences on population—Bucharest, 1974, Mexico City, 1984, and Cairo, 1994; the World Summit for Children—New York, 1990; the Earth Summit in Rio, 1992; the Vienna Conference on Human Rights, 1993; the Copenhagen Social Summit, 1995; plus a number of smaller conferences.

These conferences are designed to draw world attention to the area under consideration and produce "consensus" documents which will provide guidelines for national and international action. The documents are not enforceable documents, but they are considered to have a moral authority because they are supposed to represent a consensus of world opinion. Given its massive debt, the U.N. might find better ways to use its scarce resources, but in principle there is nothing wrong with having an international conference to focus world attention on a particular area of concern. Unfortunately, these conferences have been easy targets for those who want to use the U.N. to serve their particular ideological agendas.

41

The platforms go through a series of drafts before being presented for debate at the actual conference. Several preliminary committee meetings or PrepComs are held before the conference, where work on the platform is begun. Regional conferences held in various parts of the world offer input. The U.N. staff writes a draft and submits it to the delegates at the final PrepCom, which is held in New York. Then, the government representatives discuss the draft and try to eliminate as much controversy as possible before the actual conference. Sections where agreement is not reached are "bracketed" (enclosed in square brackets [ ]) and only the bracketed sections can be debated at the conference. The diplomats' ideal would be a conference without controversy—an expensive photo-op to prove that something wonderful had been accomplished.

U.N. conferences operate under a system of consensus. While voting is theoretically possible, a vote is almost never taken. The system was designed to protect the rights of small countries and to build popular support for programs. In the past, consensus on the wording of agreements, treaties, conventions, and documents such as conference plans of action was achieved by long and careful negotiations. This meant that whenever a nation had objections to a given word, phrase, or concept, discussions to refine the language, find synonyms or definitions continued until each nation was satisfied. If, after prolonged negotiations, a nation could not be prevailed upon to agree to the consensus, its delegation could, during the final session of the actual conference, register reservations to those sections of the document with which it disagreed.

In past years, "reservations" to a consensus had been extremely few and usually on technicalities. Those items on which consensus could not be achieved were normally dropped from the final document. This was the reason for the years of protracted meetings, and it is why U.N. assemblies are so loath to take things to a vote. A vote would be a frustration of the idea of consensus.

It should be, therefore, a source of concern that during the recent series of conferences—particularly, since the Rio summit on the environment—the system of consensus has come under attack. Certain forces within the U.N. system—namely a coalition from Western nations, U.N. agencies, and accredited Non-Governmental Organizations (NGOs)—have been determined to push policies in a predetermined direction and force their agenda into the text. Their agenda includes pushing for the legalization and expansion of abortion, various "sexual rights," and other items on the feminist agenda. As a result, the number of reservations has escalated.

In Rio at the end of the Earth Summit, the prime minister of Norway, Mrs. Gro Haarlem Bruntdland (who had chaired the conference) called for abandoning the system of consensus, because the slower countries are impeding the progress of those who wish to advance more quickly. It was well known that Bruntdland was distressed that abortion and other elements she favored had not been inserted into the text.

In Beijing, the system of consensus was essentially abandoned as the leadership forced through its agenda and told dissenting nations that if they did not agree with a particular wording, they could make a reservation.

NGOs

To assist its deliberation, the U.N. accredits representatives from national and international Non-Governmental Organizations (NGOs) who lobby government delegates. The NGOs have grown in power and influence with the U.N. bureaucracy and outnumber government delegates. To further increase NGO participation, the U.N. began authorizing forums to be held in conjunction with international conferences where the representatives from NGOs present workshops and organize caucuses to focus their lobbying effort.

The NGO movement was supposed to bring the voice of grassroots groups and international charities into the discussions, but the NGO movement has been taken over by groups which have failed to achieve grassroots support and see the U.N. as a way to achieve through lobbying what they could not in elections. Many of the NGO groups have permanent offices

in New York and paid lobbyists. In particular, the well-funded
population-control lobbyists have gained tremendous influence
at the U.N. Refugees from the sixties have found a haven at the
U.N., where they are busy pushing old causes with old rhetoric
as though the conservative tide sweeping through the U.S. and
other countries were just a bad dream. Among these are U.N.
junkies, who enjoy being where the action is, aging sixties'
peace marchers, promoters of new age religions, one-world
government advocates, and radical environmentalists. They have
been joined by feminists whose postmodernist ideology was
cultivated in the hothouse of campus academia and militant
lesbian activists. The most important of these refugees is former
U.S. Congresswoman Bella Abzug.

Bella had been elected to Congress in 1970 from a Man-
hattan district, but she had higher ambitions. Active in the
antiwar movement and other left-wing causes, she saw herself
as speaking for all women. In 1977 she chaired the First National Women's Conference in Houston. After being defeated
in several attempts to run for higher office and unable to regain
her old seat, she retreated to the U.N. where she ingratiated
herself to the U.N. bureaucracy by always being available to
give a speech or serve on a committee.

In 1990 the Women USA Fund organized WEDO, the
Women's Environment and Development Organization, "a
global information and advocacy network" with Bella as head
[Mim Kelber, "Institutions: the Women's Environment and
Development Organization," *Environment*, Volume 36, Number 8 (October 1994), p. 43]. The organization's name reflects
the fact that the first target of WEDO was the Rio conference
on the environment. WEDO's influence changed the focus of
the conference to its agenda—abortion and women's empowerment. Since Rio, WEDO has continued to manipulate the
conference process to push its agenda and turn every issue into
a women's issue.

WEDO is well funded and well connected. According to
WEDO officials: "WEDO has received recognition and support from various sources including MacArthur, Ford, Noyes,

and Turner Foundations, as well as from United Nations agencies, governments, and individual donors. Its core budget for 1994 is $630,000 with additional funds being raised for special programs" [Kelber, "Institutions," p. 43].

As the leader of WEDO, Bella Abzug was appointed to the NGO advisory committee for the Rio conference. Bella's experience was crucial to WEDO's development: "Drawing on the political and legislative skills she had developed as a women's rights advocate in the U.S. Congress, Abzug introduced an activist methodology for NGO women" [Kelber, "Institutions," p. 44].

WEDO has been instrumental in the organization of lobbying caucuses. Caucuses critique the text, circulate their recommendations for changes, and organize lobbying efforts. The largest and most important of the caucuses, the Women's Caucus, supposedly represents the interests of all women, but, in fact, is under WEDO control. WEDO also dominates a number of the other caucuses, as profamily NGOs discovered when they tried to participate in caucus deliberation.

The WEDO-controlled Linkage Caucus claims to be working to assure that the commitments made at previous conferences to the WEDO agenda are not weakened by subsequent conferences. The Linkage Caucus has, needless to say, no interest in protecting profamily commitments. The WEDO rule appears to be: Everything previously approved at U.N. conferences that they agree with is sacred, and everything that they disagree with can be changed.

During the PrepComs, Bella was in her element. Never seen without her signature hat, she rallied the Women's Caucus and spoke at U.N.-sponsored press conferences. There were persistent rumors about her health, and her admirers wheeled her around to spare her undue strain, but she could walk if she had to.

The real work of WEDO goes on behind the scenes. WEDO has become a shadow U.N. In Cairo, Bella was overheard claiming that she had written the Platform for Action. She insisted that Beijing would be her conference.

IPPF

The battle for the soul of the U.N. has been going on since its founding; however, for purposes of this discussion, the final PrepCom for Cairo held in New York in March of 1994 provides a good starting point. While a small number of prolife groups have for a long time been concerned about the influence of International Planned Parenthood Federation (IPPF) and other population groups within the U.N., the results of the PrepCom for the Cairo conference on population raised their consciousness. Pope John Paul II, alarmed over the proposed platform, wrote a personal letter to every head of state in the world listing his concerns. He also spoke strongly and frequently on the dangers of the Cairo conference. As a result, many leaders in Latin America, Africa, and the Moslem world became concerned.

The pope's efforts would have been in vain, however, if it had not been for the courageous action of Sra. Marta Lorena Casco, the government representative from Honduras, and Cecilia Royals from the National Institute of Womanhood. These women's work assured the bracketing of the most offensive parts of the text.

At the previous conference on population held in Mexico City in 1984, the Reagan administration had fought for language which would keep the U.N. from promoting abortion. The Mexico City language reads: "Abortion shall not be promoted as a method of family planning." This language had been used to restrict funding to the International Planned Parenthood Federation and other abortion provider groups.

IPPF was determined that Cairo would be their conference. They were convinced that in Cairo they could: 1) engineer the removal of the Mexico City language, 2) have abortion declared a human right as part of the newly created category of sexual and reproductive rights, and 3) receive commitments for $17 billion of new funding for their "family planning" programs around the world.

U.N. Population Fund (UNFPA) might be running the conference, but IPPF was so deeply involved in the planning and organization of the Cairo conference, that one of the pro-family delegates quipped that IPPF and UNFPA had been in bed together for so long that they qualified as a common-law marriage.

The Clinton administration came into office deeply committed to promoting abortion rights, including the repudiation of the Mexico City language and resumption of funding for abortion around the world. With the U.S. government no longer opposing their agenda, IPPF and its allies believed they would be able to roll over any opposition.

Population Control

At the U.N., IPPF has worked closely with WEDO. There had been tension between feminists and the population control movement, caused by the coercive methods used in many parts of the world to achieve population reduction. Third World women complained to Western feminists that IPPF and other population groups promoted policies which coerced poor women to accept sterilization, IUDs, and dangerous and experimental drugs. Third World feminists reminded their Western sisters that freedom of choice means the right to choose abortion and contraception, not be forced into it by overzealous population planners.

Third World feminists also documented massive abuses. In Latin America, women in labor are pressured to sign a paper agreeing to be sterilized. Many women report being sterilized without their consent during Cesarean sections. In Mexico and Kenya, women are so afraid of being involuntarily sterilized or given an IUD without their knowledge that they avoid government-run health programs.

Major donors of foreign aid, such as the World Bank, USAID, and UNFPA, routinely tie aid to acceptance of programs that promote sterilization, the IUD, and chemical contraception. Kenyan doctors reported having closets full of condoms and cases of IUDs provided by Western donors, but no latex gloves for surgery or simple antibiotics.

Contraceptive methods not considered safe for Western women are marketed in poor countries. Not only has the IUD been linked to pelvic infections and infertility, but this risk is increased when women lack basic sanitation and access to prompt medical care. Third World women are frequently recruited to test new forms of contraception, often without informed consent. The IUD and hormonal forms of contraception frequently cause excess bleeding during the woman's menstrual periods, increasing the risk of iron deficiency in women who are already undernourished. Doctors are given funds to insert the Norplant contraceptives, but not to remove them. Women who suffer from severe nausea or continuous bleeding often cannot afford to have the Norplant removed.

A pediatrician from Latin America, who was so afraid of retaliation that she asked not only that her name not be printed, but that the name of her country also be concealed, told of repeated use of foreign aid to pressure women to accept the insertion of IUDs or sterilization. She said that when she signed up for a program to encourage breast feeding, she discovered that the program was actually a way to gain the confidence of new mothers so that they could be pressured into accepting "modern" methods of contraception. She also told of how, in the rural areas of her country, the program that provides free milk for children is linked to population control. To qualify as a milk distributor, the doctor had to agree to insert a certain number of IUDs. The grant for the program includes money for the doctor to keep records to prove he has filled his quota and filed reports with the funding organization. This inevitably leads to abuses. Many women report having IUDs inserted without their consent. The pediatrician said that she was so concerned that the mothers she worked with would be pressured during labor into agreeing to sterilization that she made a point to be present to protect the rights of her patients.

Permanent forms of contraception can have tragic effects in areas of abject poverty where children are a woman's only social security. The high infant and child mortality rate can result in a situation where a woman who bears three or four children may not see any of them live to adulthood. If a woman who is pressured into agreeing to sterilization or rendered infertile by an IUD after the birth of one or two children loses her living children, she is often deserted by her husband and left without any resources or hope for the future.

Germaine Greer, one of the original leaders of the feminist movement and author of *The Female Eunuch*, wrote an entire book, *Sex and Destiny*, to document the population control movement's abuse of women in poor countries. She asks,

> Why should we erect the model of recreational sex in the public places of all the world? Who are we to invade the marriage bed of veiled women? Do we dare drive off the matriarch and exterminate the peasantry? Why should we labor to increase life expectancy when we have no time or use for the old? Why should we care more about curbing the increase of the numbers of poor than they do themselves? Who are we to decide the fate of the earth? [Germaine Greer, *Sex and Destiny* (New York: Harper & Row, 1984), p. xiv]

The population lobby has reacted to the bad publicity by claiming it has toned down its coercive programs, but reports from the field indicate that little has changed. However, the populationists have recognized that their emphasis on providing contraception and sterilization did not result in lower birth rates unless it was combined with increased female education and employment. Therefore, the population lobby now puts added emphasis on programs for increasing women's education and women's employment outside the home.

Contraceptive Imperialism

Many in developing countries no longer believe the populationist line. Mercy Walbin from *Eco-News*, Kenya, complains that the population programs being promoted in Africa are not living up to the promises made for them:

> We have successfully reduced our population to an average of 3 children from 4. . . . Our reduction in population is not matched by a corresponding improvement in our economy. In fact things are worse. . . . You can take the women to the hospital and put in as many

IUDs as you want. This makes me want to cry. The
donors are just interested in demographics, not the person. The morale in the medical field is very low. One
doctor says he can't go on. The patients can't afford to
fill their prescriptions. He has to go into his own pocket
to buy medicine in serious cases. Our shelves are full of
the pill and condoms and IUDs but medicines are not
available.

Elizabeth Sobo, who writes and lobbies to draw attention
to the economic exploitation of Africa, insists that Africa is not
overpopulated, but underpopulated. Africa's low population
density means that roads are so lightly traveled, they sometimes
revert to jungle or are covered with sand. Low population density
increases the cost of providing basic services to outlying areas.
Sobo points out that Africa isn't poor, but rich in natural resources and agricultural products. It is bankrupt because developed countries pay low prices for its products and the people
are taxed to pay interest on the debt borrowed by corrupt regimes whose leaders are now basking on the Riviera. Much of
the money borrowed went back to the donor countries to pay
for projects that had little or no effect on improving the lives
of people. Many African nations have already paid interest
equal to the principle borrowed and still owe the original amount
and more interest every year. In order to pay their debts, countries have been forced to cut health and education funding. At
each of the recent conferences, the debtor nations have begged
for debt relief, and at each they have been turned down. Funding for population control, however, has been increased.

What has also increased is the cynicism of people from
Africa and Latin America, many of whom now view the massive funding for population control as a calculated move to
impoverish their countries. A number of African and Latin
American diplomats have suggested privately that the population programs are not designed to promote the welfare of people
in developing countries, but to preserve the power of the developed countries. The developed countries of the West and Asian
rim all have birth rates which are below replacement. Given
current trends, their populations will begin to decline early in

the next century. (The reason for the current increase in population in the developed world today is increased life expectancy. Fewer people are being born, but more people are living into their eighties and nineties.)

Population growth in developing countries is slowing, but it is still above replacement. Some argue that increased population in the developing world could fuel economic development. If this happened, these countries would no longer be a market for Western goods, but would begin to produce goods for export. They would no longer be forced to sell their natural resources and agricultural products at cheap prices. Large populations in developing countries would mean that they would be able to field large armies, thereby shifting the balance of power in the world. In light of this, support for population control by rich countries looks less like humanitarian compassion and more like a means by which the rich countries intend to insure their continued economic and military dominance.

Cairo PrepCom

The PrepComs are held at the U.N. building in New York. The main committees meet in the large conference rooms on the lower level of the U.N. building. The rooms look out over the East River and are equipped with simultaneous translation systems and galleries for observers.

During PrepComs the basement of the U.N. is a bustle of activity. Tables in the corridors and inside the meetings are covered with piles of literature from NGOs, materials from national delegations, and official U.N. publications. The walls and doors display notices of caucuses, workshops, and meetings. Tight security requires NGO representatives to wear special identification badges, pass through metal detectors, and have their bags x-rayed every time they enter the building.

At the PrepCom for Cairo, the forces pushing for the population agenda were determined to brook no interference. Sra. Casco, with all the charm and style so characteristic of Latin American women, made it clear that she had no intention of surrendering to pressure. She insisted that the pro-sexual and reproductive rights language in the draft platform be placed in brackets. The U.S. delegation tried various forms of intimidation to force Sra. Casco and other profamily delegates into submission. At one point, the U.S. delegation invited her to a meeting in one of the rooms in the basement of the U.N., apparently hoping to intimidate her. When she realized their intention, she simply got up and left.

Pressure was also put on the Honduran government, including veiled threats that U.S. and U.N. aid would be withheld if Sra. Casco did not keep quiet. Sra. Casco refused to back down, insisting that she was merely defending her country's prolife, profamily constitution and laws against proabortion, antifamily language proposed for the platform. Women from the National Institute for Womanhood, a Washington-based grassroots, volunteer women's group, supported Sra. Casco's stand. NIW's president, Cecilia Royals, and Mary Suarez Ham, sister of the former Miami mayor and mother of eleven, had come to New York to support prowoman, profamily policies. As the pressure on Honduras grew, Cecilia called on friends to send faxes to the president of Honduras to let him know that there were many people who supported Marta Lorena's courageous stand.

The personal attacks on Sra. Casco backfired. The representative from Benin was so offended by what he considered to be ungentlemanly and rude treatment directed toward Sra. Casco, that in the heat of the debate he intervened and told the chair to bracket whatever Sra. Casco wanted bracketed. As a result of Sra. Casco's courageous stand, the draft went to Cairo with the most offensive sections still open for discussion.

Four

Cairo

The conference on population began the first week in September, 1994. No rain had fallen in Cairo since March—which is normal for this desert city—and the trees of Cairo looked like giant dusty artificial plants. It was rumored that Cairo was chosen as the site for the U.N. population conference to impress upon the participants the horrors of living in an overcrowded Third World city. If this was the intention, it failed. Cairo may be hot, poor, and dusty, but it pulses with life and excitement. Tourism is Egypt's number one business, and the Egyptians know how to treat guests. The hotels were well run, the food fantastic, and, for those who took time off from the proceedings, the tourist sites fascinating. The Egyptian people were very aware of the issues being debated. The waiter at the Flamenco hotel summed up the Egyptians' attitude to the population conference by saying, "Yes, they will come and talk, it won't affect us. Next year there will be a million more Egyptians."

In the weeks before the conference, the Western media had reported threats from Islamic extremists who considered the conference an affront to Islamic principles. A number of people canceled their travel plans. Some profamily attendees wrote their wills. Others came ready to die if that was what was required. To their surprise they found that the Egyptian people were universally friendly, the streets safe, and the conference well run. A woman who left her pocketbook in a church went back an hour later to find it untouched. After a hard day of lobbying, they could retire to beautiful world class restaurants, look out over the Nile, and watch the setting sun turn the city's ever-present haze wild shades of red and purple.

Alerted by John Paul II, profamily, prolife people from around the world had decided to attend the Cairo conference. It was not an organized effort, just concerned individuals from the U.S., Canada, Guam, the Philippines, Kenya, and the countries of Latin America. A young man from Canada happened to have two weeks vacation and the money, so he decided at the last minute to come to Cairo to see if there was anything he could do. A Canadian doctor and his wife came because he was Egyptian by background and felt that his knowledge of the language might help. Since many profamily people decided to come after the deadline for applying for NGO status, they asked local papers and sympathetic periodicals to send them as correspondents. Many arrived knowing almost no one and not sure what they could do, but, as the days passed, they were able to make contacts and coordinate their efforts.

Typical of the profamily forces was Dee Becker from Delaware, who decided at the last minute to come to Cairo. When she arrived, she saw an immediate need for coordination among the profamily forces. Appropriating a table in the press lounge, she set up shop, took messages, watched briefcases, and distributed flyers.

The conference was held in a modern well-appointed convention center, the NGO Forum at a large sports center, which is part of the same complex. The entire complex backed up on the street where Anwar Sadat was assassinated, and the pyramid-shaped monument dedicated to Sadat could be seen from the convention center. Although the buses avoided driving by the reviewing stand where he was shot, the taxis did not—a grim reminder that violence was always a real possibility.

The Egyptian government took the threats from Moslem extremists seriously. Security was extremely tight. All the entrances to the conference complex were equipped with x-rays and metal detectors. Streets in front of the hotels used by delegates were barricaded, and the entrances guarded. Soldiers were stationed every hundred yards along all the major highways, and a guard with a small machine gun rode on every conference bus. In spite of the precautions, or perhaps because of them, there was no sense of danger. In fact, as the conference progressed, it was clear that the only threat to American citizens would come from their own representatives.

During the conference the head of the U.S. delegation, Tim Wirth, ordered U.N. guards to arrest Keith Tucci, a pro-life activist, who was covering the conference for a South Carolina newspaper. On the word of a feminist activist, Tucci was falsely and absurdly charged with involvement in the murder of an American abortionist. He and two other Americans, whose only offense was to follow the police when they arrested Tucci, were held in custody for twenty-four hours by Egyptian police and threatened with immediate deportation. It took the intervention of Congressman Chris Smith to win their release.

The Egyptians had been led to believe that all Americans dressed immodestly, believed in sex outside of marriage, and promoted abortion and lesbianism. Tour guides, student aids at the Forum, Egyptian press, and delegates were surprised and pleased to discover profamily Americans.

Stereotypes existed on both sides. Many of the profamily NGOs had little or no previous contact with Moslems. They discovered that contrary to the stereotypes, women in Egypt were not silent, uneducated captives of a repressive antiwoman religion. Wearing a scarf over their hair did not prevent Egyptian women from using their heads. Fifty percent of Egyptian reporters are women. Typical of these is Manal Abdel Aziz, a reporter for the *Egyptian Gazette*, a Cairo English language newspaper. Tall, dark, and beautiful, Manal explained with a sweet smile that Moslem women covered their hair because a woman's hair is her most attractive feature and distracts men from her professional skills. Manal conformed to Islamic requirements for modesty, but her long sleeves, ankle-length skirts, and scarf did not prevent her from dressing with style and grace. She was not only stunning in a long-sleeved peach jacket, with a peach print skirt, and matching scarf secured by pearl-tipped pins, but extremely professional, as she worked to present an accurate picture of what was happening at the conference to her readers. Her sympathies were clearly with the profamily NGOs. Like most Egyptians, she opposed abortion, sex outside marriage, and homosexuality. She was particularly disturbed that Moslem women were being used by outside groups to promote abortion and behavior condemned by Islam.

One of the groups whose activities concerned Egyptians was the Religious Consultation on Population, Reproductive Health and Ethics, whose board included Catholic dissident Dr. Daniel Maguire (professor of ethics at Marquette University) and Frances Kissling of Catholics for a Free Choice. Funded by the Ford Foundation to promote population control, the Consultation brought together religion scholars sympathetic to its point of view on population control, contraception, and abortion. According to Maguire, the people at the Ford Foundation used to be wary of involving religion, but now believe "you have to get into the religious imagination of the people."

Maguire admitted interest in recruiting Moslem women scholars to their cause since, according to him, "secular feminists do not have nearly the amount of influence that religious feminists have in these various Moslem countries" [Mary Ann Budnik, "Interview with Daniel Maguire," 31 August 1994].

The Cairo NGO Forum

Imagine an International Planned Parenthood conference being held in the same facility as a prolife rally, while in the same building members of religious cults in strange costumes are spreading their message, Moslem women are protesting Western interference in their culture, and merchants have set up a bazaar, and you will have some idea of the atmosphere of the Non-Governmental Organizations Forum held in conjunction with the Cairo conference. The participants could browse through the booths, pick up shopping bags full of free literature, visit the food stands, or attend press conferences, caucus meetings, and workshops.

Each morning at the NGO forum, Bella Abzug presided over the Women's Caucus. Cecilia Royals and other women from the National Institute of Womanhood, believing that the Women's Caucus should be open to all women, challenged WEDO control by being the first in line whenever the microphones were opened for comments. At one point, one of Bella's assistants whispered that they had better not open the meeting for questions because the "antiabortion" people were at the microphones. She didn't know that her comments were picked up by the simultaneous translation system and could be heard by everyone who had earphones on.

NIW's profamily intervention drew applause from the Moslem participants, who soon became very vocal in their opposition to the feminist domination. During the press conferences, profamily press dominated the microphones, asking pointed questions and presenting alternate points of view. They were joined by members of the Egyptian press, who were particularly interested in challenging anyone who distorted Islamic teachings. The spokesmen for the U.N. became so frustrated that they demanded to know what publication each speaker represented. In spite of the harassment, prolifers with credentials from small-town newspapers stood their ground, while representatives from major publications had to wait their turn.

While the majority of the workshops were conducted by population control organizations and feminists, those run by profamily groups were very well attended. The Egyptian students working as aids at the forum were particularly interested in hearing about the profamily movement, and many were so enthusiastic that they joined profamily groups. The workshops were also attended by a number of Egyptian professional women, including many doctors, who were looking for information on the real problems they face, such as handicapped children, nutritional deficits, care for the dying, and maternal health. They found little of value at the populationist and feminist presentations.

Profamily participants in the forum made a point of attending the populationist and feminist workshops and speaking up to contradict the idea that contraception and abortion

were the solution for Third World women. In this regard, a
group from Kenya was particularly effective. So effective, in
fact, that the population control forces in Kenya tried to find
a way to use pressure to silence them.

SIECUS

The workshop on sex education sponsored by SIECUS
(Sex Information and Education Council of the U.S.) caught
my interest. According to the schedule, Debra Haffner, the
executive director of SIECUS, was attending the conference. I
was familiar with Ms. Haffner because several years before, I
had written a letter to the editor of the *New York Times* in
response to a column promoting condoms for teen-agers, which
said in part:

> In the debate over condoms in the schools, condom
> advocates have been avoiding the central question: Should
> children have sex? . . . Pregnancy and disease are not the
> only effects of child sex. People who are outraged over
> child molesting wink at child sex. How can those hand-
> ing out condoms know whether or not the users are
> psychologically equipped to deal with sexuality? Indeed,
> many experts believe that no child is ready to deal with
> sex, no matter how eager he or she may be to engage in
> it. . . .
>
> Condom advocates say sex is responsible as long as no
> one gets hurt. In child sex someone always gets hurt. [10
> October 1991]

Ms. Haffner sent a letter in response, where she said, among
other things, that "having sexual relations is normative behavior for teenagers 15 to 19 years old" [(30 October 1991), A24].

Since sexual relations with fifteen-year-old girls constitutes
statutory rape, I was very interested to see if Ms. Haffner would
defend this point of view in Cairo, but she did not make the
presentation. Instead the meeting was led by a young man
from SIECUS and a tall thin, black man who said he represented the MacArthur Foundation, which he said was proud to
fund SIECUS's work.

About thirty-five people were in attendance, including a number of Egyptian students who were working as aids for the forum. The spokesman for SIECUS presented the standard SIECUS line: That sexual activity is a normative way for adolescents to express themselves and that what is important is that the young people be "responsible," i.e., use condoms. The young man promoted the benefits of masturbation and outercourse (mutual masturbation to climax). A lovely young Egyptian student, whose English vocabulary did not include these terms, asked for an explanation. Since the young woman's experience clearly did not include the behaviors referred to, the explanation offered only added to the confusion.

At this point, I must admit that I became outraged at the presentation and made that clear to the SIECUS spokesman, asking him how he dared to come to Egypt and try to corrupt the innocence of these students with ideas which were destroying the young people of our country. I tried to explain to the audience the effect of the programs promoted by SIECUS. When he insisted that I sit down and allow others to speak, I protested that I could not bear to listen to a defense of the indefensible and left the room. Over half the audience followed me into the corridor where we continued the discussion. The man from the MacArthur Foundation followed the group into the hall and tried to convince the participants to return to the workshop.

In front of the Egyptians, I asked him why his organization funded a group that promoted sex for unmarried teenagers, abortion, and homosexuality—things which are rejected by most Egyptians. When the man defended his organization, the Egyptians began to argue with him.

Sexual and Reproductive Rights

Reading the draft platform for the conference and the materials distributed by population control groups at the forum, and listening to the speeches, one would believe that all that is needed to eliminate poverty, empower women, and save the world from eminent disaster is free contraception, legal abortion, and sex education to indoctrinate women and children on how to avail themselves of these "health services."

WEDO mounted a massive campaign for sexual and reproductive rights and health, arguing that every human being has a right to life, which includes a "right to health," which includes sexual and reproductive health. Therefore, if unsafe abortion is a major threat to the health of women, women's right to health would include the right to safe abortion, and, for abortion to be safe, it has to be legal. Following this twisted path, they arrived at the conclusion that the right to life gives women the right to legal abortion.

To back up their claim, they produced statistics which inflated the number of deaths from illegal abortion. An African doctor said if these figures were to be believed, all deaths in his country for women fifteen to forty would be attributable to illegal abortion, which certainly was not the case. The question of the right to life of the unborn human being was not considered.

To further confuse the question, the feminists linked sexual and reproductive health with sexual and reproductive rights even though there is no necessary relation between the two. Their version of sexual and reproductive rights would include the right to engage in various behaviors, some of which are extremely unhealthy. The Universal Declaration of Human Rights defends the right to marry and form a family, not sex for the unmarried and adolescents.

Those pushing for recognition of sexual and reproductive rights already had a foot in the door. The following statement had been approved in Mexico City in 1984: "All couples and individuals have the basic right to decide freely and responsibly the number and spacing of their children and to have the information, education and means to do so." While at the time this may have seemed like a safe compromise, profamily delegates had no idea it would be used to justify lesbians and single women having babies by artificial insemination and homosexual men using surrogate mothers.

The statement carries the implication that people have a right to a child, when no such right exists. Married people have a right to the acts which could result in the conception of a child. It is children who have a right to be born in a family where they are loved and cared for by both their biological parents.

These new "rights" were promoted at a series of workshops where a booklet entitled "Sexual and Reproductive Rights and Health as Human Rights: Concepts and Strategies; An Introduction for Activists" was distributed. The booklet, by Rhonda Copeland of the International Women's Human Rights Law Clinic at CUNY (City University of New York) and Berta Esperanza Hernández of the International Women's Human Rights Project of the Center for Law and Public Policy, St. John's University (NY), called on activists to push the idea that human rights had evolved and that "sexual and reproductive rights" were already included among recognized human rights. Just as in the U.S., the Supreme Court had "found" a right to abortion, they evidently were hoping that the Cairo conference would find "sexual and reproductive rights" in previous documents and grant them an international version of the *Roe v. Wade* decision.

The booklet defines sexual and reproductive rights as including: "respect for women's bodily integrity and decision-making as well as their right to express their sexuality with pleasure and without fear of abuse, disease, or discrimination. It requires access to voluntary, quality, reproductive and sexual health information, education and services" [Rhonda Copeland and Berta Esperanza Hernández, "Sexual and Reproductive Rights and Health as Human Rights: Concepts and Strategies; An Introduction for Activists" (Cairo: *Human Rights Series*, 1994), p. 2].

Those familiar with feminist literature know that this would include not only the right to contraception of all kinds and abortion on demand, but also legal recognition of lesbianism, sexual freedom for adolescents, sperm banks for lesbians and unmarried women, voluntary prostitution, and the prohibition of prolife demonstration. If these are declared human rights, the feminists believe they would have a powerful tool to enforce their agenda. The authors explain that their strategy is predicated on the respect due to human rights:

Human rights constitute limitations on the sovereignty
of states; they constitute principles to which states, donors, providers, intergovernmental organizations and
ultimately, the private economic sector must be held
accountable. [Copeland and Hernández, p. 1]

Human rights do not depend on whether a state has
acknowledged them, for example, by ratifying a particular treaty. Widely endorsed human rights norms are
relevant regardless of whether a state has ratified a particular treaty. [Copeland and Hernández, p. 3]

Human rights are standards to which everyone is accountable, but they cannot be expanded to serve an ideological agenda.
Human rights must be founded on the truth about the human
person.

Copeland and Hernández accuse "religious fundamentalists" of opposing their human rights: "This demand for el-
emental human rights is being met with opposition by religious
fundamentalists of all kinds, with the Vatican playing a leading
role in organizing religious opposition to reproductive rights
and health including even family planning services" [Copeland
and Hernández, p. 3].

Religious leaders, including Archbishop Renato Martino,
the delegate of the Holy See to the U.N., reject the feminist
claim that religious groups oppose human rights. Martino,
however, makes a clear distinction between real human rights,
which are inherent to the person, and attempts to manipulate
the idea of human rights:

Currently, there is a tendency to believe that society has
formulated what are known as human rights. However,
human rights are such precisely because they are inherent to the dignity of the human person. A society may
acknowledge or violate human rights, but it cannot
manipulate the existence of human rights, since these
rights precede even the state. [November 1994]

Those who follow the U.N. have been very concerned that
the feminists and their allies will try to use the fiftieth anniversary of the signing of the U.N. Declaration of Human Rights
in 1998 to push for a rewriting of the document. "A Proposal

for a Universal Declaration of Human Rights from a Gender Perspective," circulated by CLADEM (*El Comite Latinoamericano y del Caribe para la Defensa de Los Derechos de las Mujers*), suggests that the declaration be rewritten to guarantee rights for "children, homosexuals and lesbians, bisexuals, transsexuals and hermaphrodites." The following provisions would be added:

> All persons have the right to free and responsible sexual education that guarantees the right to their own sexuality.
>
> All persons have the right to their sexual orientation which includes the decision to take or not take an emotional and/or sexual companion who belongs to the same or a different sex.
>
> All women and men ought to be guaranteed the right and have the full power to autonomous decisions over their reproductive functions. Such rights include but are not restricted to: a) access to health services; b) free and voluntary maternity and paternity; c) family planning; d) access to safe methods of contraception; e) voluntary interruption of pregnancy in safe conditions; f) voluntary sterilization of men and women; g) sexual autonomy; h) life free of violence in the exercise of sexuality and especially of pregnancy.
>
> All men and women have the right to different forms of physical, sexual, emotional, and spiritual pleasure that are an essential part of the human condition. This right includes whatever possibilities of responsible sexual pleasure exist within the context of the person, the couple, the family, and the community. ["Propuesta Para Una Declaración Universal de los Derechos Humanos Desde Una Perspectiva de Género" (Lima, Peru: CLADEM) pp. 7-8, translation from Spanish by the author]

María Ladi Londoño echoed the same sentiments in an article entitled "Sexuality and reproduction as human rights," published by the Latin American and Caribbean Women's Health Network. "The Universal Declaration of Human Rights has fallen short of its purpose," according to her. "Humans must have new rights with symbolic, real or even rhetorical meaning" [María Ladi Londoño, "Sexuality and reproduction as human rights, Women and Population Policies (Oaxtepec, Mexico: Latin American and Caribbean Women's Health Network, 5-9 July 1993), p. 66]. Londoño lists the various problems, including "imposed child-rearing," "heterosexual orientation as the universal model," and "the conditions in which the great majority of sex workers live," which she believes would be addressed by promotion of sexual and reproductive rights [Londoño, p. 68]. Londoño believes that "once recognized as universal, sexual and reproductive rights, finely tuned through the process of acceptance, will become a part of the dynamics of liberation and personal growth" [Londoño, p. 73].

In trying to use human rights to forward their agenda, the feminists are embarking on a very dangerous course. The Western nations might be able to use their economic power to enforce their "expanded" version of human rights on the rest of the world and pressure poor countries into legalizing abortion and gay rights. What is more likely, however, is that Western pressure to "expand" human rights will undermine respect for human rights in developing countries.

In many parts of the world, human rights are just beginning to mean something and women are just beginning to take advantage of that still-fragile respect accorded human rights. Setting up a false conflict between religion and human rights could jeopardize that process and put the most vulnerable—including women and girls—at risk.

The Egyptian Solution

In the ten years since the Mexico City conference, IPPF had been forced to labor under the restrictions imposed by the Mexico City language. Now, with Reagan and the Republicans out of power and President Clinton committed to their cause, IPPF believed that this was their moment of triumph. One hundred twenty-eight of their employees were to be included on national delegations. Twenty-two members of Planned Parenthood, including their president, had been appointed to the U.S. delegation. The chairman of the main committee was Dr.

Fred Sai of Ghana, the president of IPPF. The delegates were supposed to represent their national interests, but during the conference, they held closed meetings to plot strategy.

At the crucial point in the deliberations at the conference, Dr. Sai tried to make it appear that the Vatican was blocking the consensus on proabortion language. The media headlined the charge. In fact, no consensus on abortion had been reached. Moslem countries publicly opposed the promotion of abortion, as did a number of Latin American countries. Other less vocal countries were pleased with the Vatican leadership, since it allowed them to avoid having to incur the wrath of donor nations by speaking publicly.

The sides were sharply divided, and at one point it appeared the process would break down. The Egyptians, in an attempt to save the conference, suggested a compromise: the language on sexual and reproductive health would remain in the text, but a *chapeau* (covering paragraph) would be placed at the beginning of the document guaranteeing national sovereignty and protecting religious values. While this solved the immediate problem, it set a dangerous precedent.

The prosexual and reproductive rights crowd could then argue that "fundamentalists" were using religion to oppose human rights. The platform also stated clearly that the conference was not authorized to grant new human rights. The Mexico language was not repudiated. Instead, the phrase "in no case shall abortion be promoted as a method of family planning" appeared in the platform in two separate places.

To the detriment of the conference, the battle over sexual and reproductive rights had occupied center stage. Profamily delegates had no time to focus on chapter 4, "Gender Equality, Equity and the Empowerment of Women," which called for "women's equal participation and equitable representation at all levels of the political process and public life" and "gender equality in all spheres of life, including family and community life." Since the profamily forces enthusiastically supported women's equal rights, most saw no danger in these sections. Totally occupied with what for them were life and death issues, they were not interested in looking for new problems.

Cairo woke up the profamily movement to the dangers of an activist U.N. They had an opportunity to meet like-minded people from around the world and form working relationships. In particular, it provided a moment for Christians and Moslems to recognize that the old stereotypes and misunderstandings hid their basic agreement on the importance of family, life, and faith. Although a number of Evangelical Christians had come to Cairo as individuals, the major groups were not well represented, something a number of people came to believe needed to be remedied in the future.

Profamily forces achieved a great victory in Cairo, however, by averting an almost certain international *coup d'état* by Planned Parenthood and its allies. The profamily forces had been able to hold the fort against an advancing enemy, but at the end of the battle, their enemy had not surrendered a single inch of territory, and, although they didn't realize it at the time, the profamily cause had lost a great deal in Cairo. "Gender" and "sexual and reproductive rights and health" had found their way into a U.N. document. Once accepted, no matter how many qualifications were attached, they would pose a problem.

As the conference drew to an end, Bella Abzug and her friends, who had declared at the beginning that this was their conference, were frustrated and angry that they had not been able to win acceptance of abortion as a human right. They retreated to the bazaars and tourist attractions for which Cairo was famous, to soothe the sting of their defeat, with the promise, "Wait until next year. What we didn't get there, we will win in Beijing."

Five

Conspiracy at Glen Cove

The profamily coalition left Cairo determined to organize and prepare for the Beijing conference on women, but they were already two years behind their opposition. Two PrepComs for Beijing had already been held, and several drafts of the platform produced. An entire bureaucracy had for many months been directing its energies toward Beijing.

Preparations for the NGO forum included the publication of a regular newsletter. The September 1994 issue reported that women NGOs were already actively lobbying for the inclusion of a gender perspective in U.N. documents. Another article reported on a panel discussion at which Maria Suarez of the Latin American Women's Health Network, in what was described as a "moving" speech, attacked "religious fundamentalism" and demanded that "Beijing should expose them to the world for what they are doing to women" ["NGO Forum on Women '95 Bulletin," (September/October 1994) p. 4].

The bulletin also provided information on an international petition campaign designed to "put Sexuality on the Agenda at the World Conference on Women." Launched by the International Gay and Lesbian Human Rights Commission, the campaign "aimed at mobilizing support for inclusion of sexual orientation in the Platform" [p. 8].

Regional Conferences

The preparations for Beijing included regional conferences held in Vienna, Austria; Mar del Plata, Argentina; Amman, Jordan; Dakar, Senegal; and Jakarta, Indonesia. WEDO literature promoting the conferences claimed that "WEDO will work to ensure full access by grassroots women to national and regional governmental and NGO preparatory meetings" ["WEDO FACT Sheet"].

WEDO's definition of grassroots women appears to be limited, however, to women who agree with them. Profamily women's organizations were neither informed nor invited, and those who did discover the conferences found obstacles in the way of their participation. The regional conference for U.S. women was held in Vienna—hardly convenient.

At the Vienna regional meeting, the conference chairman, Johanna Dohnal, condemned the rise of extreme right-wing political parties. According to Dohnal, these parties were part of a "male-bonding culture" whose message to women was "stay in their homes and take care of the children." A.P. Melkert, minister of Social Affairs and Employment of the Netherlands, called for changing the images of masculinity and femininity.

The statement issued by the Vienna Regional Preparatory meeting included several references to the Gender Agenda, in particular the following sections:

> Sec. 2(c): Partnership between women and men is the basis for a new gender contract based on equality which would entail a redistribution of the domestic and family care, contribute to economic independence for women, reduce women's double workload and break down existing stereotypes of the roles of women and men.
>
> (d) A new gender contract involves an active and visible policy of mainstreaming a gender perspective into all relevant political, economic and social policy fields at central, regional and local levels.

Mar del Plata

The regional conference and NGO forum for Latin America met in Mar del Plata, Argentina. Dorotea Vedoya, Cristina

Delgado, and Rita Barros de Sverdlik were among a small group of profamily women who, in spite of various forms of harassment, participated in the associated NGO meetings. These women charged that the organizers of the NGO forum purposefully manipulated the arrangements to exclude the participation of profamily women. The forum received little publicity. The meetings, locations, times, and themes of the workshops were not announced ahead of time. A number of large nonfeminist women's organizations were denied credentials. Those who were able to attend found that their contributions were ignored, and, in spite of assurances to the contrary, their statement of dissent was not included in the report to the secretariat. They did, however, have a chance to observe the gender feminists close up and in action.

During the workshops, speakers insisted that women should liberate themselves from the vocations of wife and mother and from the traditional concepts of marriage and the family. In a workshop on "Myth and Sexuality," the presenter insisted that "the right to choose" extended to other areas of sexual liberty, such as prostitution, and that incest was acceptable unless it involved the use of power by an adult over a child.

The International Association of Lesbians and Homosexuals (*Asociación Internacionál de Lesbianas y Homosexuales*) were active participants in the workshops. A member of that organization, Rebeca Seville, in a workshop on "Democracy and Citizenship," insisted that she and her lover had the right to establish a family with all the same rights as other families.

In Mar del Plata the profamily participants also encountered the writings of Marta Llama, a well-known Mexican feminist. Of particular concern were Sra. Llama's comments on gender and her claim that there were more than two sexes. According to Sra. Llama,

> Biology shows that, outwardly, human beings can be divided into two sexes; nevertheless, there are more combinations that result from the five physiological areas which, in general and very simple terms, determine what is called the biological sex of a person: genes, hormones, gonads, internal reproductive organs and external repro-

ductive organs (genitals). These areas control the five
types of biological processes in a continuum. . . . A quick
but somewhat insufficient classification of these combi-
nations obliges one to recognize at least five biological
sexes.

men (persons who have two testicles)

women (persons who have two ovaries)

hermaphrodites or herms (in which there are at the
same time one testicle and one ovary)

masculine hermaphrodites or merms (persons who have
testicles, but present other feminine sexual characteristics)

feminine hermaphrodites or ferms (person with ovaries,
but with masculine sexual characteristics)

This classification functions only if we take into account
the internal sexual organs and the "secondary" sexual
characteristic as a unity; but if we imagine the multiple
possibilities that could result from a combination of the
five physiological areas that we already mentioned we
see that our dichotomy man/woman, more than a biological reality, is a symbolic and cultural reality. [Marta
Llamas, "Cuerpo: Diferencia sexual y género" from Cristina
Delgado "Definiciones estraídas de documentatos usados
en Foro Mar del Plata," pp. 2-3, author's translation]

According to Sra. Llama, man/woman, masculine/femi-
nine are merely cultural constructions, and thinking that heterosexuality is the "natural" sexuality is only another "example
of a 'biologized' social construction."

The tragedy of congenital deformities does not prove there
are more than two sexes and certainly doesn't prove that heterosexuality is not natural, any more than the fact that some
babies are born blind proves that it isn't natural for human
beings to see. Biological sex isn't determined by external organs, but by genetic structure. Every cell of the human body is
clearly marked male or female. What is absurd is that a number
of feminists found this argument convincing.

The profamily delegates found Sra. Llama's reasoning difficult to follow, but her point was clear: male and female is something people have made up; therefore, homosexuality is equal to heterosexuality:

> The non-existence of a feminine or masculine essence allows us to exclude the supposed superiority of one sex over the other and also even to question if there is a "natural" form of human sexuality. . . . In certain circles psychoanalytical reflection is arriving at a slow acceptance of homosexuality as an equal option to the psychological condition of heterosexuality. In other words, one may say that heterosexuality is the result of a psychic process, or even that it is not "natural." [Marta Llamas, quoted by Delgado, p. 3, author's translation]

Sra. Llama's frequent references to gender and her definition of gender as "the symbolization that each culture establishes over sexual difference" led the profamily participants to believe that "mainstreaming the gender perspective" was a covert means to promote radical feminist ideology and homosexuality. The following statement from the Mar del Plata forum report did nothing to allay those concerns:

> Heterosexism attempts to make heterosexuality the norm and so not only maintain inequality between us women ourselves and the violence against lesbians, but also helps maintain inequality between women and men, by prescribing that every woman who would be normal ought to be with a man, even a man who attacks her, violates her and denies her pleasure. [Foro de ONG de America Latina y El Caribe, Mar del Plata, 20-24 Setiembre, 1994 Paz: El Derecho a una Vida sin Violencia. (*Coordinadoro de ONG's de America Latina y El Caribe.* Foro de ONG's Beijing '95), p. 5]

Unfortunately, most of this material was available only in Spanish and only to a limited audience. The Argentineans' strong concerns were not taken seriously even by many profamily delegates. Furthermore, the concern about gender was diminished even among the Spanish-speaking delegates because when the Platform for Action draft was issued, the Span-

ish version did not translate the word *gender* as *genero*, the
Spanish equivalent, but *sexo* [sex].

Women's Global Strategies Meeting

In preparation for the Beijing conference, WEDO held a
three-day Women's Global Strategies meeting, 30 November
to 2 December 1994, in Glen Cove, New York. WEDO was
so confident of its control of the process that it distributed a
complete report of the meeting and posted a list of the participants on the Internet.

Ten percent of the women participating in the Glen Cove
meeting were U.N. employees, including Gertrude Mongella,
secretary general of the Beijing conference, and Kristen Timothy, who was in charge of accreditation of NGOs.

Gertrude Mongella, of Tanzania, has a long history of ties
with WEDO. She is a member of their International Policy
Action Committee, and she appointed WEDO to act as an
Expert Advisory Group on three issues: (1) women and environment development; (2) increasing women's participation in
decision making; (3) and consensus building [WEDO FACT
Sheet]. Kristen Timothy's participation raised a number of
questions, since a large number of profamily, prolife groups,
some of whom had participated in previous U.N. conferences,
were initially denied Non-Government Organization status for
the Beijing conference by her office.

Since the purpose of the Glen Cove meeting was to plan
a strategy for influencing the outcome of U.N. conferences and
to attack policies supported by member nations, the presence of
so many paid U.N. employees, even if only as observers, constitutes, at the least, a serious conflict of interest for the U.N.
staff. It also lends credence to charges that the U.N. bureaucracy is far more sensitive to the concerns of the feminist NGOs
than to protecting the rights and interests of the member nations. Actions like these lend credence to the charges that the
U.N. is an unregulated and out-of-control bureaucracy. The
report issued by WEDO after the meeting targeted the groups
considered obstacles to their agenda:

Monitor and oppose internationalization of anti-abortion and other fundamentalist movements. . . . Counter Holy See and fundamentalist movements' efforts to weaken and reverse gains made in Cairo during preparations for the Social Summit and the 4th World conference on Women. . . . Counter religious extremists/ Fundamentalism and re-claim the moral space/family values/family concerns. ["Women's Global Strategies Report," WEDO, December 1994]

For feminists the term *fundamentalists* is not restricted to Moslem extremists or Protestants who hold to biblical inerrancy. At a panel discussion conducted by NGOs during the Beijing PrepCom entitled "Counter Attack: Women Stand up to Fundamentalism," speakers labeled Catholics, Evangelical Christians, Eastern Orthodox Christians, Moslems, prolifers, anyone who believes in the complementarity of men and women, and those who support motherhood as a special vocation for women, as "fundamentalists."

Under this definition of fundamentalism, the majority of the member states could be classified as "fundamentalist," since their people, laws, constitutions, and customs support "fundamentalist" religion, motherhood, and the right to life. The U.N. Universal Declaration of Human Rights defends freedom of religion, motherhood, and family. The participation of U.N. staff in a meeting so directly opposed to the interests of so many member states, and to the principles on which the U.N. was founded, brings into question the ability of the U.N. staff to perform ethically and fairly.

Besides U.N. staff and members of various feminist organizations, the participant list included representatives from the Ford Foundation, the MacArthur Foundation, Planned Parenthood, CNN, and the Body Shop (a chain of stores selling herbal/natural soaps and personal products).

Diane Faulkner from the U.S. Department of Labor was also listed as a participant. Ms. Faulkner's participation in a meeting whose goals, among other things, included achieving fifty/fifty, male/female quotas for the government and private sector by the year 2005, raises questions, since the Clinton administration has repeatedly denied accusations that it supports quotas. The Glen Cove report records no opposition to the following targets:

> Governments should achieve 50% inclusion of women in elected and appointive office by the year 2005.
>
> Influential economic actors such as private corporations and financial institutions, trade unions, international financial institutions such as the World Bank and IMF should increase the number of women in key positions to 50% by the same time.
>
> This should be achieved by: a) setting numerical and affirmative action goals, including quota systems; and b) establishing mechanisms' to monitor and demonstrate progress toward achieving that goal. [Working Group 6, "Women's Global Strategies Report," p. 2]

The participants in Glen Cove recognized that merely increasing the number of women in elected and appointed offices would not achieve their goals. According to the report, they want assurances that "women leaders elected and appointed to decision-making positions be accountable to the concerns, demands and platform articulated by women around the world through the Beijing process" [Working Group 4, "Women's Global Strategies Meeting," p. 8].

An anecdote from a female graduate student at MIT offers an insight into how feminists work to insure that the right kind of women are placed in key "decision-making" positions. The student, who was considering various career possibilities, attended a talk on women in the U.S. Environmental Protection Agency, where she was treated to an insider's view on how feminists use power. The woman from the EPA, obviously believing she was among like-minded women, explained in great detail how she had maneuvered herself into a position of power within the EPA and was now in charge of hiring for her department. She explained that she was careful to review resumes of potential employees and to look for clues of politically correct activities because, as she put it, she wanted to make sure that she didn't just hire "some lucky woman."

Other disturbing programs promoted by Glen Cove included safe abortion "as a basic method of fertility regulation and as an essential part of reproductive health services"; the recognition of "sexual orientation as a fundamental human right within the context of the expanding definition of the family"; and educating men and women toward the transformation of gender roles.

Promotional Video

If Mongella's attendance at the Women's Global Strategies Meeting constituted a conflict of interest, she showed even worse judgment by appearing in a video created to promote the NGO forum. The video, *Breaking Barriers*, attacks the world's major religions as antiwomen, strings together half-truths and distortions, rehashes old accusations, and promotes the radical feminist interpretation of history. While defending goddess worship and witches, it reminds the viewer that for women "under Hitler it was children, the kitchen and the Church." Complaints about the mistreatment of women are accompanied by pictures of a cathedral. The following excerpts from the video reveal the antireligious tone:

> In ancient Rome and Egypt goddesses were linked to fertility and to the creation of life and thus, worshipped, but nothing has done more to constrict women than religious beliefs and teachings. . . . Orthodox Jews still thank God in their prayers for not having made them women. . . . Christianity or, rather, its interpretation has made its own contribution to the subjection of women. . . . It's the issue of women and witchcraft which St. Augustine labeled "Hell's black river of lust." It's the stubborn position of a Christian parish that prefers to go without priests than allow women into this exclusive male stronghold. . . . John Stuart Mill, who had been actively involved in women's rights in the 19th century, called marriage a school of despotism.

The video did not just malign Christianity. Other religions were also insulted:

In Arab Islamic society, the status of women has been
relatively unchanged throughout the centuries. Women
have been subordinate to men because the society has
always been patriarchal. A man could marry four wives
and still keep concubines. . . . Together with other major religions of the world, Chinese beliefs including Con-
fucianism, Taoism, and Buddhism have been discriminatory to women.

While the video ends with a commitment to "inclusiveness
and full participation of all," nowhere in the video was the pro-
religion point of view presented. Women who believe that religion has promoted the well-being of women were not included among those interviewed.

Although the video was produced by an independent company without U.N. funds, the appearance of Mongella and use
of the copyrighted conference logo gave the impression that it
was an official U.N. production. The video's creator, Judith
Lasch, said that the video had been shown to the U.N. staff
and NGOs and that everyone, including Gertrude Mongella,
was very pleased with it.

Such attacks on religion are, unfortunately, all too common at the U.N. If the fault line at the U.N. used to be
between Communist and democratic regimes, the new fault
lines appear to be running between aggressively secularist states
and those which support religious values. While the secularists
claim that the religiously orientated states are impeding consensus, in fact, it is the secularists who are determined to enforce their world view in every corner of the world.

An unintended effect of this attack on religion has been
the growing cooperation among religious peoples. Finding
themselves on the same side in the battle for family, life, and
faith, people of different faiths are discovering how much they
have in common. Recognition of shared values and increased
understanding between religious groups may be one of the
most positive results of this series of conferences.

Six

The World According to Bella

PrepCom for Beijing

While the media focuses on the conference, the PrepCom is where the real work is done. Ideally, the U.N. staff would like to see all the controversial problems solved before the cameras are turned on. Then, the conference would simply be a coronation of their latest plan to save humanity from the disaster currently under discussion.

When the PrepCom for Beijing convened in March of 1995, the draft Platform for Action had already undergone numerous alterations. The delegates were supposed to have received copies of the newest version of the platform on 1 February, but the unofficial text was not made available until 17 February. On 27 February, sixteen days before the PrepCom was scheduled to begin, the participants received the official 70 page, 246 paragraph text. Those who had tried to prepare ahead of time by studying the previous drafts found that their work had been in vain. This text had been radically altered and completely renumbered.

Profamily government representatives and NGOs sifted through pages and pages of repetitive language and pious platitudes looking for anything that might endanger family values. They found many areas of concern. Even after the PrepCom began, they were still uncovering potential landmines in the text. Of even more concern was what was not there. The draft platform ignored the needs of women who work at home and had nothing positive to say about marriage, family life, motherhood, parental rights, or religion. The text's sheer size, however, forced profamily NGOs to focus their lobbying efforts on the most offensive sections. To further complicate the process, the translations into Spanish and French concealed the antifamily agenda. Since English is the official text, profamily delegates from Latin America and French-speaking Africa were at a disadvantage. Also, many of the delegates were unfamiliar with the ideological implications of the English words. Non-English speakers relied on dictionaries, which rarely, if ever, carried the new definitions invented by postmodernist deconstructionist feminists. Honduran representative Marta Lorena Casco worried about a "hidden agenda" and accused U.N. insiders of using "manipulated euphemisms to draft a text for which they had the only dictionary."

Many of the delegates and NGOs arrived in New York exhausted. They had spent January in New York at the PrepCom for the Social Summit, February in Copenhagen at the Social Summit, and were now back in New York for the Beijing PrepCom. Some had flown directly from Copenhagen to New York without returning home for a break. They had no time to study the text and little opportunity to strategize with like-minded delegates.

WEDO and its allies came fully prepared and ready to oppose all profamily amendments and push for their agenda. The profamily coalition, which had formed in Cairo, had made a good showing at the PrepCom for the Social Summit in Copenhagen. Through their intervention, the language on family had been strengthened

While only a few profamily groups had the resources to send representatives for the entire meeting, which dragged on for almost four weeks, a number came for shorter periods of time. More people had intended to come, but, at the last minute, a large number of profamily groups who had applied for NGO status were inexplicably denied accreditation. The U.N. issued a statement saying that because of the large number of national applications, only groups whose activities were relevant to the conference were accepted. This made no sense, as three of the largest, most relevant, and national groups—Concerned Women for America, Eagle Forum, and Catholic Campaign—were denied and Catholics for a Free Choice, a nonmembership organization with fourteen employees, funded by rich foundations was approved for NGO status. The battle over accreditation continued until August.

Catholics for a Free Choice

The PrepCom began with a shock. To the surprise of everyone, on the first day, Sheri Ricket, of the Vatican delegation challenged the accreditation of Catholics for a Free Choice and its Latin American affiliates on the grounds that CFFC is not a Catholic organization. CFFC president Frances Kissling was outraged.

At the Cairo conference, Kissling had been omnipresent, using every opportunity to criticize the Catholic church. She spearheaded a petition drive to have the Holy See's permanent observer status at the U.N. revoked. The Vatican dismissed the petition as a propaganda ploy, but they were concerned about CFFC's distortions of Catholic teaching in Latin America. During the PrepCom, Kissling distributed a paper entitled "Equal is as Equal Does," which she coauthored with Mary Hunt, of WATER (Women' Alliance for Theology, Ethics and Ritual) for Women-Church Convergence. The Kissling/ Hunt paper called for "a feminist anthropology" based "on the radical equality of women and men," where "community, rather than family is the 'programmatic focus.'" Hunt will be remembered for her participation in the radical feminist Re-Imaging Conference, in Minneapolis in 1993, where she proposed substituting friendship as a metaphor for family:

> Imagine sex among friends as the norm. Imagine valuing genital interaction in terms of whether and how it fosters friendship and pleasure. . . . Pleasure is our birthright of which we have been robbed in religious patriarchy. . . . I picture friends, not families, basking in the pleasure we deserve because our bodies are holy. [Re-Imaging Conference, quoted in *HLI Reports* (January 1995), p. 6]

Since family relationships—God as Father, Jesus as Son—
are at the very center of the Christian faith, replacing *family*
with *friendship* isn't just a change of metaphor. Hunt's views on
sexuality put her outside Christian tradition. Feminists are, of
course, free to leave established faiths, but they are not free to
demand that revealed doctrines be changed to fit their behavior.

Kissling countered the Vatican charges by arguing that
CFFC had never claimed to be representatives of the Catholic
church. But, there was substantial evidence that CFFC had
tried to give the impression that they were providing "Catholic"
advice. A CFFC pamphlet offered "abortion facts from Catholic teaching to Catholic attitudes and practices. Meditations for
before and after abortion respond to women's spiritual needs."
Another CFFC pamphlet is entitled "Reflections of a Catholic
theologian on visiting an abortion clinic." A third, "A Guide to
Making Ethical Choices," which answers such questions as "Is
abortion murder? How do I make a decision?" was written by
Marjorie Reiley Maguire and Dr. Daniel Maguire.

Marjorie Maguire has since repudiated CFFC. In a letter
to the editor of the *National Catholic Reporter* she supported
the Vatican's charge that CFFC was not a Catholic organization, pointing out that while its members may have been bap-
tized Catholic, they neither attend Catholic services nor believe
in even the most basic Catholic teachings [Marjorie Reiley
Maguire, Letter to Editor, *National Catholic Reporter* (21 April
1995)].

In order to save its accreditation as an NGO, CFFC issued
a press release which said, "Our name does not imply that our
organizations are 'official' Catholic organizations and we have
never made such a claim. We are an organization of Catholic
people, not the church." A letter was sent to the U.N. stating
the same. This statement was precisely what the Vatican wanted.
Their goal was not to prevent CFFC from participating in
Beijing, but to force CFFC to admit it was not a Catholic
organization.

Tibetan Women

The Chinese delegation blocked accreditation of NGOs representing Tibetan exiles. Kissling tried to identify her situation with that faced by the Tibetan women by inviting them to join her press conference. There was, however, no comparison. The Vatican's request that apostates not masquerade as true believers can hardly be compared to the cultural and physical genocide Tibetan women have suffered under Chinese domination.

The Chinese have instituted a draconian population program in Tibet, even though Tibet has never had a population problem. Tibetans are a deeply religious people, and, before the Communist Chinese invasion, a substantial portion of the population entered celibate monastic life. As part of the program to solidify their control of Tibet, however, the Chinese have forced Tibetan women to undergo abortions and sterilization, imprisoned and raped Buddhist nuns, closed monasteries, and interfered with religious freedom. Tibetan women in exile came to the PrepCom to draw attention to these abuses. The Tibetans presented massive evidence of the denial of religious freedom in Tibet, including this account of the torture of a Buddhist nun:

> I was stripped naked and made to lie face down on a cold concrete floor. They beat me with a rope and stick and with an electric prod. They beat me as I lay fully stretched out on the floor. I thought at that time I was about to die. The picture of Guru Rinpoche appeared before my eyes and then I fainted. In order to make me come to, they threw cold water on me. They were very insulting. They squeezed my breasts saying that there was much milk in them; that I was no nun, that I had had at least two children already. They said that I was having sexual relations with the monks and that is why we were demonstrating together. I said that I was a nun. They pushed a stick in my vagina again and again hurting me so much that for three days I could not urinate. One of the guards pushed an electric cattle prod into my

anus and left it there. It was like a pain came into my
heart that was unbearable. I fell unconscious. [International Committee of Lawyers for Tibet, "Denial of Tibetan Women's Rights to Freedom of Religious Belief
and Expression" (San Francisco, CA, 10 March 1995),
p. 7]

The press release handed out at the press conference also
contained personal accounts of how women had been forced to
have abortions, or like Lh, who fled Tibet, forcibly sterilized:

> When the Chinese officials came to my house after the
> birth of the third child, they told me I would not get a
> ration card for the third child and that I had to pay a
> fine. They informed me that I had been put on a list of
> women who would soon be sterilized. Again, I did not
> protest. I knew it would be useless to try to negotiate
> with them. Many of my friends were in the same position and were either sterilized or aborted. We simply
> had no choice. [International Committee of Lawyers for
> Tibet, "Denial of Tibetan Women's Right to Reproductive Freedom" (San Francisco, CA, 1 March 1995), p.
> 10]

The press release also included an eyewitness report of the
work of Chinese mobile birth control teams in Tibetan villages
in 1987:

> The villagers were informed that all women had to report to the tent for abortions and sterilizations or there
> would be grave consequences. For the women who went
> peacefully to the tents and did not resist, medical care
> was given. The women who refused to go were taken by
> force, operated on, and given no medical care. Women
> nine months pregnant had their babies taken out. . . . We
> saw many girls crying, heard their screams as they waited
> for their turn to go into the tent, and saw the growing
> pile of fetuses build outside the tent, which smelled
> horrible. During the two weeks of this mobilization, all
> pregnant women were given abortions, followed by sterilization, and every woman of childbearing age was sterilized. [p. 9]

The Tibetans who came to New York to plead for international intervention were unaware that they were being used by their feminist supporters to promote "reproductive rights." The press release which denounced the terrible abuses of Tibetan women included the following recommendation:

> That Tibetan women be provided with access to health care facilities to ensure availability of safe and effective birth control methods, safe abortions and sterilizations, should Tibetan women choose such options. (p. 14)

A woman from the National Institute of Womanhood (NIW) took one of the Tibetans aside and asked how her group as Buddhists could support abortion. The Tibetan was shocked. She had not been aware that proabortion language had been included in the press release and had no idea that in the West, "reproductive rights" meant the right to abortion. She had thought that it meant the right to have a baby. The Tibetan cause was ignored by the national delegates.

The Coalition for Women and the Family

The profamily participants at the PrepCom for Beijing renewed friendships made in Cairo and organized themselves as the Coalition for Women and the Family. First-timers were introduced to the U.N. system. The coalition ran their lobbying effort from the leather benches just outside the room where the negotiations were going on.

The location allowed access to electric outlets into which coalition members plugged in their portable computers and printers. This allowed the coalition to respond quickly as the debate unfolded. They monitored the debate, and, when an issue arose, one person would write a flyer. Someone else would proofread it. Others would check it to be sure that there was nothing in it that could be misinterpreted. Someone would check with friendly delegates, if any could be found, to obtain their reaction. The flyer would be translated into Spanish and French, and another version written, making similar points for Moslem delegates, and then runners would go off to find a copy machine where the versions would be printed on brightly colored paper. The use of colored paper allowed those handing out the flyers to tell at a glance whether or not a person had received a particular flyer. At times, one could look down from the gallery and tell by the colors that almost the entire body was reading the latest flyer.

The coalition had no formal organization or funding. Everything was strictly ad hoc. It worked because of the dedication and expertise of the members. Some, like Jean Head of International Right to Life, had years of experience at the U.N. Jean worked nights as a nurse so she could lobby during the day. For Brenda Alexander, a black minister's wife from Memphis, it was her first experience in international politics.

The technique was so successful that the U.N. staff was continually finding rules in a rulebook, which no one ever saw, to restrict the distribution of flyers and otherwise limit the activities of the coalition. The Coalition for Women and the Family adapted quickly to the changing rules, however, much to the consternation of the WEDO crowd, who complained loudly during their caucuses about the "fundamentalists" who were trying to sabotage the PrepCom. While coalition members were frequently barred from the floor during the formal sessions, Bella Abzug sat in the seat of an absent delegate. She received preferential treatment and still complained that the NGOs didn't have enough power.

WEDO members accused the coalition of wanting to keep women at home and subordinate to men, which was absurd, since coalition women were at the U.N. working with men without any struggle or quotas, domination, or subordination. The women in the coalition considered themselves living proof that the profamily movement supported the participation of women in politics. As single and married women, working women and full-time mothers, they believed they represented the real aspirations of women.

At one point, several members of the lesbian caucus tried to muscle the coalition off the benches where they normally met by sitting on their coats and papers and obviously trying to overhear their conversations. Olivia Gans of American Victims of Abortion tried to make friends with them and engage them in meaningful conversation. Eventually they went away.

The PrepCom was contentious from the beginning. At one point, a single paragraph of text had generated thirty-two pages of amendments. The representatives disagreed about abortion, parental rights, debt, migration, the universality of human rights, unrenumerated labor, prostitution, whether the discrimination against women began at birth or before, and a host of other issues.

Gender Perspective

For the Coalition for Women and the Family, the immediate threat was the language on sexual and reproductive rights and health and parental rights. A few were concerned about the repeated use of the word *gender* in the draft and references to "mainstreaming the gender perspective," "gender analysis," "gender aspects," "gender concept," "gender sensitivity," and "gender roles." Most of the profamily delegates and NGOs, however, assumed that *gender* was just a polite substitute for *sex*.

The concern about gender was sufficient, however, for the coalition to prepare the following flyer to draw attention to the question, which read in part:

What is Gender Perspective?

Gender perspective may be a strange term for some delegates. It does not mean "commitment to women's rights" or opposition to "discrimination on the basis of sex." It means seeing everything as a power struggle between men and women. Each problem is analyzed in terms of how the differences between men and women are the *cause* of the problem.

The problems are, of course, real and serious. Individual men are often guilty of great injustice to women, but the gender perspective sees *all men* as guilty and benefiting from the "power" inequalities. Statistical differences between men and women are seen as proof of a male plot against women. All the suffering of women is somehow the fault of men.

DELETE THE ANTI-MALE LANGUAGE
WHAT IS NEEDED IS THE WOMEN'S PERSPECTIVE

Coalition for Women & the Family

While the gender issue was not a priority among pro-family delegates, the supporters of the "gender perspective" were incensed that anyone would challenge the gender perspective.

In response to questions about the definition of *gender*, the conference leadership floated the following definition: "Gender refers to the relationships between women and men based on socially defined roles that are assigned to one sex or the other."

Rather than solving the problem, this definition only served to create more confusion. The delegate from Malta expressed reservations about the proposed definition. As a lawyer, he failed to see how laws could be written about relationships based on socially defined roles. Laws, he insisted, must refer to male and female human beings. Several delegates began bracketing *gender* each time it appeared in the text.

Bella's Speech

The reaction to the suggestion that *gender* be bracketed was swift and belligerent. It revealed that those who were concerned about the ideological implications of the word *gender* had, in fact, underestimated the importance of this term. On 3 April, Bella Abzug was given a special opportunity to address the delegates. In an angry speech, she condemned attempts to bracket the word *gender* until a definition could be agreed upon: "We will not be forced back into the 'biology is destiny' concept that seeks to define, confine and reduce women to their physical sexual characteristics."

The delegates to the PrepCom were shocked by the accusation that defining *gender* as a synonym for *sex* was an attempt to confine or reduce women to their physical sexual characteristics. Bella insisted the "feminist" definition of *gender* was universally understood and accepted, which was certainly not the case:

> The concept of *gender* is embedded in contemporary social, political and legal discourse. It has been integrated into the contemporary social, political, and legal discourse. . . . The meaning of the word *gender* has evolved as differentiated from the word *sex* to express

the reality that women's and men's roles and status are socially constructed and subject to change.

Bella acted as though the delegates were totally aware of the contemporary discourse about "sex" and "gender." In fact, most of the delegates had been, until this moment, blissfully ignorant of the ideological trajectory of feminist thought. According to Bella, "The infusion of the gender perspectives into all aspects of UN activities is a major commitment approved at past conferences and it must be reaffirmed and strengthened at the Fourth World Conference on Women."

The delegates, many of whom had attended previous U.N. conferences, began to scan U.N. documents for evidence that they had approved a definition of gender as socially constructed roles that can be changed. They found that the 1948 Universal Declaration of Human Rights had referred to *sex*, not *gender*. The 1985 Nairobi Forward Looking Strategies used the word *sex* and spoke about "women's perspectives." The 1993 Declaration on the Elimination of Violence against Women used the word *gender* several times, but there was no hint of a new definition. Nor had the participants at Cairo been aware of any new definition.

In her speech, Ms. Abzug insisted that her definition of *gender* was non-negotiable:

> The current attempt by several Member States to expunge the word *gender* from the Platform for Action and to replace it with the word *sex* is an insulting and demeaning attempt to reverse the gains made by women, to intimidate us, and to block further progress. We urge the small number of male and female delegates seeking to sidetrack and sabotage the empowerment of women to cease this diversionary tactic. They will not succeed. They will only waste precious time. We will not go back to subordinate inferior roles.

The delegates were not interested in pushing women back into "subordinate inferior roles." Everyone was committed to promotion of the equality and rights of women. They only wanted to understand what the word *gender* meant before they

approved a text where the word appeared over two hundred
times.

Seven

Reimagining Gender

To add to the controversy, a member of a government delegation who had considered the debate about the definition of *gender* an overreaction, mentioned the topic to the family's baby sitter. The baby sitter just happened to be taking a course at Hunter College entitled "Re-Imagining Gender." She explained to her employer that Bella was correct. *Gender* no longer meant *sex*, but referred to socially constructed roles. The baby sitter provided copies of the course materials to prove this. These were photocopied and circulated among profamily delegates and members of NGOs.

The students had been assigned a two- to five-page paper on their own "reimagining of gender," and the course's instructor, Lorna Smedman, had written the following introduction for her students:

> In this course, we will read a variety of texts—modernist and postmodernist literature, science fiction, the cartoon, film, essays—to find out how twentieth-century thinkers have reimagined the concept of gender. Is gender a "social construction" or the product of "biological sex"? What is at stake in transgressing the binary categories of female/male, feminine/masculine, heterosexual/homosexual, natural/unnatural?

The representatives from conservative countries were not interested in returning home with a document that "transgressed binary categories" or which opened up the issue of homosexuality.

Among the photocopied materials was an article by Adrienne Rich entitled "Compulsory Heterosexuality and Lesbian Existence," which included the following quotes: "heterosexuality, like motherhood, needs to be recognized and studied as a political institution" [Adrienne Rich, "Compulsory Heterosexuality and Lesbian Existence," *Bloody Bread and Poetry: Selected Prose, 1979-85* (New York: W.W. Norton & Co.), p. 35 (photocopied materials supplied for course)].

"In a world of genuine equality, where men are non-oppressive and nurturing, everyone would be bisexual" [Rich, p. 34].

An article by Lucy Gilbert and Paula Webster, "The Dangers of Femininity," suggest that defining *gender* as a "social construction" would mean that masculine and feminine are not natural, hardly a comforting thought for the delegates:

> Each infant is assigned to one or the other category on the basis of the shape and size of its genitals. Once this assignment is made we become what culture believes each of us to be—feminine or masculine. Although many people think that men and women are the natural expression of a genetic blueprint, gender is a product of human thought and culture, a social construction that creates the "true nature" of all individuals. [Lucy Gilbert and Paula Webster, "The Dangers of Femininity," *Gender Differences: Sociology or Biology?*, p. 40 (photocopied materials supplied for course)]

A chapter taken from a book by Kate Bornestein, a man who underwent a "sex-change," argues that the way to liberate women is to deconstruct gender: "Women couldn't be oppressed if there was no such thing as 'women.' Doing away with gender is key to the doing away with patriarchy" [Kate Bornestein, *Gender Outlaw: On Men, Women and the Rest of Us* (New York: Rutledge, 1994), p. 115].

For Bornestein the number of genders is not limited to two: "Gender fluidity is the ability to freely and knowingly become one or many of a limitless number of genders, for any length of time, at any rate of change. Gender fluidity recognizes no borders or rules of gender" [Bornestein, p. 52].

Particularly troubling was an article by Anne Falsto-Sterling entitled "The Five Sexes: Why Male and Female Are Not Enough." This article was the source of the ideas promoted by Marta Llamas. Ms. Falsto-Sterling claims that the existence of various genital abnormalities constitutes a reason for expanding the number of sexes from two to five—males, females, herms, merms, and ferms.

Ms. Falsto-Sterling's interest in adding extra sexes does not appear to be related to a sincere concern for the small number of individuals who suffer from these abnormalities, but from a desire to challenge traditional beliefs:

> Why should we care if there are people whose biological equipment enables them to have sex "naturally" with both men and women? The answers seem to lie in a cultural need to maintain clear distinctions between the sexes. . . . Inasmuch as hermaphrodites literally embody both sexes, they challenge traditional beliefs about sexual difference: they possess the irritating ability to live sometimes as one sex and sometimes the other, and they raise the specter of homosexuality. [Anne Falsto-Sterling, "The Five Sexes: Why Male and Female Are Not Enough," *The Sciences* (March/April 1993), p. 24]

Ms. Falsto-Sterling sees the acceptance of the existence of more than two sexes as advancing the feminist and homosexual agenda: "Imagine that the sexes have multiplied beyond currently imaginable limits. It would have to be a world of shared powers. Patient and physician, parent and child, male and female, heterosexual and homosexual—all those oppositions and others would have to be dissolved as sources of division. A new ethic of medical treatment would arise, one that would permit ambiguity in a culture that had overcome sexual division" [Falsto-Sterling, p. 24].

The articles included in the Re-Imagining Gender class were bizarre, but the profamily delegates and coalition members who read them could not help but notice that many of the themes contained in the articles were echoed in what had here-

tofore seemed to be innocent statements in the proposed Platform for Action.

Feminist Epistemology

A reporter for the "Earth Negotiations Bulletin" called the
debate over gender "a textbook case study on the state of global
feminism and feminist epistemology," which "raised central debates on the relation between language, knowledge and power,
the political contest over 'natural' and socially negotiated identity, and ideas informing the current 'backlash' against some of
the feminist advances made in the US" ["Earth Negotiations
Bulletin," 10 April 1995].

Most of the delegates, however, hadn't come to New York
to debate "feminist epistemology." The defenders of *gender*
insisted that the word had been accepted at the U.N. and in
academic literature and had not been questioned before. Those
questioning the use of gender pointed out that it had not been
questioned before because no one knew they had invented a
new definition.

When the U.S. objected to a definition of *gender* which
included the terms *two sexes*, the delegates began to speculate
on their motives. Did the representatives of the Clinton administration believe that there were more than two sexes, or
additional genders? If so, how many, and what were they? Profamily delegates were concerned that the "gender perspective"
concealed a hidden agenda, namely, the promotion of homosexuality. The Clinton administration was known to be aggres-
sive in its support of the homosexual agenda. Was their refusal
to define *gender* as two sexes part of this agenda? The discussion created a great deal of confusion. Several reporters picked
up the subject, and a number of conservative leaders in the
United States and Latin America were under the impression
that the platform promoted five genders: male, female, homosexual, lesbian, and bisexual or transsexual.

Marta Casco, as chief of the Honduran delegation, asked
the U.N. officials for a definition of gender. She was told that
gender "did not have a definition and did not need one." She

was accused of trying to sabotage the cause of women and undermine the conference by even raising the question.

Sra. Casco made a strong intervention, warning that "in the search for her legitimate rights and equality of opportunity, the woman should not surrender and even less deny her own nature" and that "to design a world of individualistic, egotistical women who are marginalized from family realities will not contribute to the eradication of violence nor the overcoming of injustices or inequalities nor the diminishing of poverty, to the contrary" (author's translation).

True Protection

Gender was not the only source of contention at the conference. Almost every paragraph generated debate. Both sides suggested additional paragraphs, eventually swelling the text by one-third. While over one hundred new paragraphs were added, those presented by profamily delegates were mysteriously omitted from the printed record of the proceedings.

For example, in the section on violence against women, the draft blamed violence on the family, religion, tradition, and "unequal power relations between men and women." Seeking to offer positive solutions to the problem of violence, profamily delegates offered the following paragraph:

> It is important to recognize that the only true protection for women is a society where men are taught from infancy that acts of violence or disrespect toward women are unmanly and unacceptable. Mothers, as the primary teachers of children and formers of consciences must raise their sons to understand that men must respect women and protect them from all forms of violence and abuse. Fathers must reinforce these teachings with words and actions.

When the printed record appeared, this paragraph was nowhere to be found. The chairman claimed that it was an oversight, but took no corrective action.

Deliberations dragged on, and, eventually, the PrepCom had to be delayed for three days. The profamily forces saw that the extension was a ploy to shift power to the richer nations, since delegates from the poorer, profamily countries, who had already made plane reservations, would have to leave with many important issues undecided.

The coalition supported the demands for a clear definition of *gender*. Although several in the group felt that the word had acquired so much ideological baggage that it should be replaced by other terms—either *male and female*, or *women's* or *sex*, as was appropriate—the profamily delegates felt that all that was necessary was to clearly define *gender* as referring to "male and female, the two sexes of the human person."

When Marta Casco, the delegate from Honduras, made a formal request that *gender* be bracketed throughout the document, the chairman, Irene Freidenschlus of Austria, in an unprecedented move, refused. Sra. Casco continued to defend her right to bracket unacceptable text. When it became apparent that the controversy could not be contained, Freidenschlus agreed to forming a contact group which would meet from 15 May to 15 June to discuss a definition of gender.

The "Earth Negotiations Bulletin" reported that the U.S. was not interested in having gender clearly defined: "Some of the most interested parties in the debate are now represented in the Contact group set up to arrive at an agreed understanding of the word gender. As one senior US delegate put it, the likely outcome will be the introduction of some 'positive fuzziness' to the text" ["Earth Negotiations Bulletin" (10 April 1955)].

The daffodils in the park in front of the U.N. were just peeking out of the ground when the PrepCom began. They had already begun to wither by the time it was over. A third of the text was still in brackets, and no decision had been made on the question of *gender*. Looking back, the profamily forces would realize that this was the high point of their influence. Behind the scenes, money and power were being used to assure the triumph of the Gender Agenda.

Part II

Part II

Eight

Radical Feminism

The month between the end of the PrepCom and the convening of the contact group on gender gave interested delegates and NGOs opportunity for a crash course on feminist theory. The "Re-Imagining Gender" course material had opened some eyes and raised many questions.

The confusion was understandable. A massive chasm exists between the public perception of feminism and the reality of feminist theory. I had faced that chasm myself, when a number of years ago, I began to research feminism. I read all the well-publicized feminist authors, but what they said didn't make sense. A piece was missing. I could hear a melody playing, but I couldn't quite recall the words.

I shared my problem with a friend, Claire Driver, who taught Russian literature at the University of Rhode Island. She just laughed and said, "Dale, they are all Marxists." Class struggle, oppression, patriarchy—I had heard it before. It had been a long time since I had read Marx, but I remembered, "All history is the history of class struggle . . . Oppressor against oppressed." The words fit the tune.

It had all been there, but I hadn't seen it. Looking back through the feminists' texts, I was amazed at how many of them quoted Marx and his companion and confidant Frederick Engels and, in particular, Engels' book, *The Origin of the Family, Private Property and the State*. I hadn't regarded it as significant when Kate Millett in *Sexual Politics* praised Engels' theories: "The great value of Engels' contribution to the sexual revolution lay in his analysis of patriarchal marriage and family" [Kate Millett, *Sexual Politics* (New York: Avon, 1971), p. 167].

I didn't realize that when Millett wrote the following explanation of the roots of "oppression" she was revealing her own ideological roots: "In the subjection of female to male, Engels (and Marx as well) saw the historical and conceptual and prototype of all subsequent power systems, all invidious economic relations, and the fact of oppression itself" [Millett, p. 169].

Nor had I noticed that Barbara Ehrenreich and Deirdre English in their book, *For Her Own Good*, included the following quote from "The Communist Manifesto": "All fixed, fast-frozen relations, with their train of ancient and venerable prejudices and opinions, are swept away, all new-formed ones become antiquated before they can ossify. All that is solid melts into air, all that is holy is profaned, and man is at last compelled to face with sober senses his real conditions of life and his relations with his kind" [Barbara Ehrenreich and Deirdre English, *For Her Own Good* (Garden City, NJ: Anchor Press, 1978), p. 5].

I had regarded Marxism as a defunct economic theory until then. My limited exposure to Marx had not included his social theory. And, in any case, to suggest that someone was a Marxist was simply not done. In post-McCarthy America, such a suggestion would bring instant shame not on the accused, but on the accuser.

But, the evidence was all there. A trip to the local feminist bookstore—a converted candy store with announcements posted outside promoting every imaginable left-wing cause—revealed that the feminist Left was further left than I had imagined. The floorplan of the store read like a roadmap of the feminist soul—the left wall was devoted to feminist literature, theory, and theology; the middle aisle to lesbianism and homosexuality; the back of the store to witchcraft, the New Age, and the environment; and the right side to the writings of Marx, Engels,

Gramsci, and their fellow travelers. I hadn't even realized that some of these works were still in print.

Knowing that the feminists followed Marx (with certain revisions, of course) did not explain the Gender Agenda. Luckily, a good friend and profamily activist, Michael Schwartz, suggested that if I wanted to understand the feminists, I should read Engels' *The Origin of the Family, Private Property and the State* and Shulamith Firestone's *The Dialectic of Sex*. In these books, I saw how the dialectic of Marx had become the dialectic of sex. Shulamith Firestone was not among the feminist media stars, but she was widely quoted by feminist authors. *Ms.* magazine listed her book among feminist classics, and it is required reading in women's studies programs. As I read through Engels and Firestone, I understood how the words fit the music.

From Liberal to Radical

The Gender Agenda attempts to build on the good will generated toward feminism in the 1960s, when the women's movement promoted a "liberal feminism" or in Christina Hoff Sommers' terms an "equity feminism." Liberal feminism holds that women should have as much liberty in society as men and insists that the individual should be considered separately from the group. So widespread was the support for liberal feminism that almost all the legislation required to outlaw discrimination on the basis of sex was passed without serious opposition. In fact, one of the arguments made against the Equal Rights Amendment was that it was unnecessary because women already had equal rights.

Contrary to the claims of the feminist Left, no one wants to reverse these gains. There is no "backlash" against a woman's right to vote, to hold office, to equal education, or to equal opportunity in employment. Women, like myself, who are adamant in their opposition to the Gender Agenda are active in the political and economic lives of their communities, expect equal rights, equal education, equal opportunities, and equal treatment.

Profamily advocates do, however, recognize the limitations of liberal feminism, particularly its failure to take into account the real and obvious differences between men and women and to recognize that many of the laws "discriminating" between men and women were not attempts to oppress women, but attempts to compensate for natural differences and protect women. When these laws were removed, women often suffered as a result of so-called equal treatment. Liberal feminism, with its emphasis on the individual, ignored the importance of the family as a social unit. Liberal feminism is also prone to an overemphasis on big government as a solution to all problems, including the problems of women.

Profamily advocates believe that it is possible to be fully committed to the equal dignity and rights of men and women without denying the differences between the sexes, de-emphasizing the family, or resorting to big government. Liberal feminism's influence eroded partially because it succeeded in its objectives, partially because its limitations became apparent, but primarily because it was superseded by a radical feminism which held that liberal feminism hadn't gone far enough. The so-called backlash against feminism is not directed against the liberal feminism of the sixties, but against the new strains of feminism, which repudiated liberal values in favor of revolutionary ideology.

According to Alison Jagger, who wrote a textbook on feminism, the radical feminists repudiate liberal feminism because liberal feminists did not recognize "that it is necessary to change the whole existing social structure in order to achieve women's liberation" [Alison Jagger, "Political Philosophies of Women's Liberation," *Feminism and Philosophy*, ed. by Vetterling-Braggin, Elliston and English (Totowa, NJ: Littlefield, Adams & Co., 1977), p. 9].

This repudiation of liberal feminism occurred in the late 1960s. The women's movement was taken over by political radicals. Neo-Marxist politics were in vogue. Women who joined revolutionary movements were exposed to revolutionary ideologies. The battle against oppression was, however, not very liberating for many of these women. Their revolutionary brothers treated women badly, relegating them to cooking, typing, and performing sexual services, while refusing to allow them to voice their opinions or have leadership positions within the movement.

The radical women rebelled against this mistreatment and, in doing so, looked to their revolutionary ideology for justification. They found exactly what they needed in the philosophy of Karl Marx and Frederick Engels, particularly in Engels' book, *The Origin of the Family, Private Property and the State.* Imagine their delight when they discovered that Marx and Engels had taught that women were the first private property and the oppression of women by men the first class oppression:

> In an old unpublished manuscript written by Marx and myself in 1846, I find the words: "The first division of labor is that between man and woman for the propagation of children." And today I can add: The first class opposition that appears in history coincides with the development of the antagonism between man and woman in monogamous marriage, and the first class oppression coincides with that of the female sex by the male. [Frederick Engels, *The Origin of the Family, Private Property and the State* (New York: International Publishers, 1942), p. 58]

The proclamation by Marx and Engels that all history is the history of class struggle is well known. What is less well known is their contention that the first class struggle occurred in the family. According to Marxist theory, in the early ages of human existence, people lived in peaceful classless societies composed of matrilinear family units where private property was unknown and oppression nonexistent. Some Marxists even hold that men did not even know they were fathers, not having made the connection between the sexual act and the subsequent birth of the child. According to classic Marxist theory, all this was changed by what amounts to the Marxist version of Original Sin: men discovered or insisted on the recognition of their fatherhood, enslaved women in marriage, created the patriarchal family, and established private property. Class strife and oppression followed. In 1884 Engels wrote: "The overthrow of the mother-right was the *world historical defeat of the female sex.* The man took command in the home also; the

woman was degraded and reduced to servitude; she became the
slave of his lust and a mere instrument for the production of
children" [Engels, p. 50].

Marx and Engels held that in order to achieve liberation
from perpetual class struggle, the means of production and
reproduction must be removed from the hands of oppressors
and restored to the workers. This would require not only the
abolition of private ownership of property but, also, the destruction of the father-headed family; that all women would be
forced to work outside the home; free day care and the collec-
tivization of household tasks; easy divorce, sexual liberation
and the acceptance of illegitimacy; and finally, the destruction
of religion because religion supports the family:

> The first condition for the liberation of the wife is to
> bring the whole female sex back into public industry,
> and that this in turn demands the abolition of the mo-
> nogamous family as the economic unit of society. [Engels,
> p. 66]

> With the transfer of the means of production into com-
> mon ownership, the single family ceases to be the eco-
> nomic unit of society. Private housekeeping is trans-
> formed into a social industry. The care and education of
> the children become a public affair; society looks after all
> children alike, whether they are legitimate or not. This
> removes all the anxiety about the "consequences," which
> today is the most essential social—moral as well as eco-
> nomic—factor that prevents a girl from giving herself
> completely to the man she loves. Will not that suffice to
> bring about the gradual growth of unconstrained sexual
> intercourse and with it a more tolerant public opinion in
> regard to a maiden's honor and a woman's shame?
> [Engels, p. 67]

The nascent radical feminists seized on the concept of
control of reproduction. Liberation would require absolute female control of pregnancy and birth, including unrestricted
access to contraception and abortion. The revolution would
also bring about total sexual liberation and liberation from the
restrictions of marriage and family.

After the Russian revolution, the Communists initially tried some of these policies, but retreated when they saw the disaster caused by a frontal attack on the family. The Communist system instead focused on socialization of industry and control of the political apparatus.

The radical women of the sixties saw in Marx's and Engels' analysis the justification of their own dissatisfaction with liberal reforms. They became convinced that previous Marxist revolutions had failed because they had failed to target the family. If Marxist analysis was correct, the family was the cause of oppression and would have to be eliminated. Marx's and Engels' writings offered substantial support for an attack on the family. Marx says that "the modern family contains in germ not only slavery, but also serfdom" [Marx, quoted by Engels in *The Origin of the Family, Private Property and the State*, p. 51]. Engels writes: "The modern individual family is founded on the open or concealed domestic slavery of the wife" [Engels, p. 65]. And, he says that the married woman "differs from the ordinary courtesan in that she does not let out her body on piece-work as a wage worker, but sells it once and for all into slavery" [Engels, p. 63].

Ellen Herman, in an article in *Sojourner: The Women's Forum*, entitled "Still Married After All These Years," writes of the early days of the radical feminist movement: "In the late '60s, the radical young women who reclaimed the derisive term 'feminist' and made it central to their own developing political identities pinpointed the family—specifically, the Western, patriarchal, bourgeois, child-centered, and nuclear family—as the most important source of women's oppression" [September 1990, p. 14s].

The early radical feminists criticized marriage as the "gender socialization process," the sexual double standard, the ideology of romantic love, and "compulsory heterosexuality." These feminists demanded "wages for housework" on the grounds that "women's liberation and capitalism were contradictory" and capitalist "profit" could occur "only when more than half of the population went unpaid for a vast amount of work." They demanded the right to abortion on the grounds that "reproductive control was prerequisite to anything resembling equality."

The Dialectic of Sex

The writer who best articulated the radical feminist vision was Shulamith Firestone. In her book, *The Dialectic of Sex*, Firestone shows how Marxism can be transformed into radical feminism:

> So that just as to assure elimination of economic classes requires the revolt of the underclass (the proletariat) and, in a temporary dictatorship, their seizure of the means of *production*, so to assure the elimination of sexual classes requires the revolt of the underclass (women) and the seizure of control of *reproduction:* the restoration to women of ownership of their own bodies, as well as feminine control of human fertility, including both the new technology and all the social institutions of childbearing and childrearing. And just as the end goal of socialist revolution was not only the elimination of the economic class *privilege* but of the economic class *distinction* itself, so the end goal of feminist revolution must be, unlike that of the first feminist movement, not just the elimination of male *privilege* but of the sex *distinction* itself; genital differences between human beings would no longer matter culturally. [Shulamith Firestone, *The Dialectic of Sex* (New York: Bantam Books, 1972), pp. 10–11]

Here is the foundation of radical feminism and the heart of the Gender Agenda: the elimination of sex distinction and control of reproduction. The radical feminists agree with the Marxists that the goal is a classless society, but the radical feminist revolution would do away with sex classes. The key to this would be "control of reproduction."

It should be pointed out—not because it matters in the grand scheme of things, but because feminists are uncommonly defensive, humorless, and easily offended—that there are several subsets of left-wing feminists, and they become very upset if you get them confused. The Marxist feminists believe that the Marxist revolution must precede the feminist revolution.

The socialist feminists believe that the Marxist and feminist revolutions must take place at the same time, and the radical feminists believe that the feminist revolution must be first. There were also Lesbian and Matriarchal Separatists who believed that the revolution required a retreat from a two-sexed society into all-female enclaves—organized either around lesbian relationships or motherhood. For our purposes it is easier to call them all radical feminists, since all these ideas could certainly be classed as radical, and the similarities among them outweigh the differences.

Firestone believes that men were able to trap women into marriage because women had all the babies, and she credits Engels with this insight: "Engels did observe that the original division of labor was between man and woman for the purposes of childbreeding; that within the family. The husband was the owner, the wife the means of production; the children the labor; and that reproduction of the human species was an important economic system distinct from the means of production" [Firestone, p. 4].

The first objective of the revolution would be to free women from the burden of childbirth. She argues that if women would simply refuse to have babies, men would have to invent a technological solution.

"The reproduction of the species by one sex for the benefit of both would be replaced by (at least the option of) artificial reproduction; children would be born to both sexes equally, or independently of either, however, one chooses to look at it" [Firestone, p. 12].

Artificial uteruses or surgical techniques which would allow males to gestate human fetuses have not yet been developed, although the idea continues to resurface. (I have yet to encounter a man interested in volunteering for this experiment.) The more moderate radical feminists, if this is not an oxymoron, retreated from this biotechnological revolution to a demand for absolute female "control of reproduction," which would include abortion on demand for the entire pregnancy, and free and easy access to all forms of contraception and all reproductive technologies.

Interestingly, Firestone always recognizes that she is attacking the "biological reality." "Unlike economic class, sex class sprang directly from a biological reality: men and women were created different and not equally privileged" [Firestone, p. 8].

"Natural reproductive differences between the sexes led directly to the first division of labor based on sex, which is at the origins of all further division into economic and cultural classes" [Firestone, p. 9].

For her this is no problem. She is willing to toss out the "natural" if it impedes the revolution: "Thus, the 'natural' is not necessarily a 'human' value. Humanity has begun to outgrow nature; we can no longer justify the maintenance of a discriminatory sex class system on the grounds of its origins in Nature. Indeed, for pragmatic reasons alone it is beginning to look as if we must get rid of it" [Firestone, p. 10].

Polymorphous Perversity

Firestone also calls for absolute sexual freedom. The family, according to Firestone, is based on the restriction of sexuality to married partners. Therefore, elimination of the family will be accompanied by liberation of sexuality from any restrictions on the number, sex, age, biological relationship, or marital status of the participants. She calls for "a reversion to an unobstructed *pansexuality*—Freud's 'polymorphous perversity'— would probably supersede hetero/homo/bi-sexuality" [Firestone, p. 12].

In order to understand the relationship between feminism and lesbianism, it is necessary to understand that there are three theories of the origin of the homosexual and lesbian orientation: innate, polymorphous, and traumatic:

Innate. People are born either homosexual or heterosexual, and there is nothing they can do about it. Homosexuality is, therefore, natural and equal to heterosexuality. Society should grant full rights for homosexuals to marry and adopt children. Sexual orientation is viewed as the equivalent of race—something you didn't choose and can't control.

Polymorphous. Human beings are born without any sexual orientation and are capable of being attracted to either sex. The sex of one's partner is irrelevant. People who hold this view believe that the categories of homosexuality, heterosexuality, and bisexuality should be abandoned so that human beings can revert to a "natural polymorphously perverse sexuality."

Traumatic. Homosexuality and lesbianism are caused by childhood psychological trauma, such as rejection by the same sex parent, sexual abuse, or a combination of factors. Homosexual and lesbian behavior is viewed as an addictive or self-destructive way of dealing with unresolved childhood problems. The condition can, in many cases, be successfully treated if the person wants to change. The homosexual and lesbian sexual orientation is viewed as similar to drug addiction or alcoholism.

While feminists tend to argue that lesbianism is innate when they are lobbying for gay rights, among themselves they talk of the choice of a sexual partner as a political statement. According to Alison Jagger, some feminists believe that, while polymorphous perversity is the ultimate goal, the present situation requires that women adopt lesbianism as a "way of combating the heterosexual ideology that perpetuates male supremacy" [Jagger, p. 15].

Profamily advocates believe that all human beings have equal rights to respect and physical safety, but oppose special rights based on sexual orientation, same sex marriage, and teaching children that homosexuality is normal.

There has been considerable debate about the influence of lesbians in the feminist movement. Some claim they dominate the movement. The election of Patricia Ireland, who has admitted to a lesbian relationship, to the presidency of the National Organization of Women (NOW) seemed to confirm that charge. There is also debate about whether lesbians are naturally attracted to feminist activism, or if women involved in feminism are recruited to experiment with lesbian sexuality. In any case, the feminist movement is strongly committed to lesbian rights, and feminist theory is used to defend lesbianism.

Children's Sexual Liberation

Firestone also calls for the total liberation of children and
the virtual abolition of childhood: "We must include the oppression of children in any program for feminist revolution. . . .
Our final step must be the elimination of the very conditions
of femininity and childhood" [Firestone, p. 104].

Firestone's comments on children's liberation show the
ideological link between radical feminism and the children's
rights movement. According to Firestone,

> The incest taboo is now necessary only in order to pre-
> serve the family; then if we did away with the family we
> would in effect be doing away with the repressions that
> mold sexuality into specific formations. All other things
> being equal, people might still prefer those of the oppo-
> site sex simply because it is physically more convenient.
> [Firestone, p. 59]

Firestone sees nothing inherently wrong with incest or
sexual child molesting: "Adult/child and homosexual sex ta-
boos would disappear, as well as nonsexual friendship. . . . All
close relationships would include the physical" [Firestone, p.
240].

She believes that absolute sexual liberation is the key to
political and economic liberation: "If early sexual repression is
the basic mechanism by which character structures supporting
political, ideological, and economic serfdom are produced, an
end to the incest taboo, through the abolition of the family,
could have profound effects. Sexuality would be released from
its straitjacket to eroticize our whole culture, changing its very
definition" [Firestone, p. 60].

Firestone, in fact, believes that once the incest taboo is
eliminated there would be nothing wrong with a child having
sexual relations with his mother.

Firestone's ideas are so extreme that it is easy to understand why the feminists—many of whom were deeply influenced by her theories—were very careful not to put her forward
as the spokesman for their movement. The radical feminists
did not forsake Firestone's vision of an absolute sex class revolution. They merely recognized that it would have to be packaged in a more acceptable form.

Nine

Really Radical Feminism

Engels was not the only Marxist who influenced feminist
thinking. The Italian Marxist Antonio Gramsci is frequently
cited by radical feminists. Gramsci, who was jailed for his views
in the 1930s, believed that the revolution had failed in Italy
because the people clung to their religious faith. According to
Gramsci, people not only believe in religion, but, because of
their religion, they believe certain things about what is natural
and what is unnatural. For him, religion is the means by which
the ruling class enforces its power and gains the people's consent to their own oppression. He believed that the revolution
had failed to win popular support because people were captive
to "hegemonic ideas":

> By hegemony Gramsci meant the promotion through-
> out civil society—including a whole range of structures
> and activities like trade unions, schools, the churches,
> and the family—of an entire system of values, attitudes,
> beliefs, morality, etc. that is in one way or another sup-
> portive of the established order and the class interests
> that dominate it. [Carl Boggs, *Gramsci's Marxism* (Lon-
> don: Pluto Press, 1976), p. 39]

According to Gramsci, religious values are just tools of the
capitalists to keep the workers in line. This theme was taken up
by socialist lesbian feminist Christine Riddiough, who argues
the family is the instrument the "ruling class" uses to suppress

women's sexuality. Riddiough is the "chair" of DSA Feminist
Commission, a group which has been active at the U.N. ["Christine Riddiough and DSA listed as part of the Cairo U.S.
Network," *Cairo '94 Bulletin*]. She believes that the lesbian
issue can be used against the "hegemonic" idea of the family as
natural:

> Gay/lesbian culture can also be looked on as a subversive
> force that can challenge the hegemonic nature of the
> idea of the family. It can, however, be done in a way that
> people do not feel is in opposition to the family per se;
> a simple "smash the family" slogan is seen as a threat not
> so much to the ruling class as to people in the working
> class who often rely on family ties to maintain security
> and stability in their lives. In order for the subversive
> nature of gay culture to be used effectively, we have to
> be able to present alternative ways of looking at human
> relationships. [Christine Riddiough, "Socialism, Femi-
> nism, and Gay/Lesbian Liberation," *Women and Revo-
> lution*, ed. by Lydia Sargent (Boston: South End Press,
> 1981), p. 87]

This idea of redefining the family surfaces again and again in
feminist literature. Publicly they claim to be profamily. They
use the word *family*, but change the meaning.

Deconstruction

Those who try to explain the current state of feminist
thought face a difficult task. Feminist theory is essentially
unstable. One can take a snapshot of the feminist movement at
any particular moment, but the situation is sure to change
before the film is developed. While this may present a challenge for those studying feminism, it is not a problem for
feminist theorists. Truth, reality, logic, scientific evidence, veri-
fiable research—these are just words to the feminists.

Radical and gender feminists believe that men made up
history, science, and religion to oppress women, and women
must remake them to achieve their liberation. History and science are seen as tools to forward the revolution. If a theory can
be implemented in a way that will give power to women, it is

accepted. For them, the question is not, "Are manhood, womanhood, motherhood, fatherhood, masculinity, femininity, heterosexuality and marriage really 'socially constructed gender roles,'? but will calling them socially constructed gender roles serve our political ends?"

Academic feminists have embraced the postmodernist/ deconstructionist theory, which holds that language is just words which impose an arbitrary structure on individual objects which have no intrinsic meaning or relationship. Words are deconstructed by proving that a word serves a political purpose, giving one group power over another. According to deconstructionist theory, once the word is stripped of its power, people will be liberated. The reality behind the words is ignored. In the end, everything can be deconstructed.

Judith Butler, in her book *Gender Trouble: Feminism and the Subversion of Identity*, suggests that if gender is socially constructed, maybe sex is also socially constructed. Judith Butler's writings are almost impossible to decipher, as the following quotes demonstrate:

> Originally intended to dispute the biology-is-destiny formulation, the distinction between sex and gender serves the argument that whatever biological intractability sex appears to have, gender is culturally constructed: hence gender is neither the causal result of sex nor as seemingly fixed as sex.

> If gender is the cultural meanings that the sexed body assumes, then a gender cannot be said to follow from a sex in any one way. Taken to its logical limit, the sex/ gender distinction suggests a radical discontinuity between sexed bodies and culturally constructed genders. [Judith Butler, *Gender Trouble: Feminism and the Subversion of Identity* (New York: Routledge, 1990), pp. 6-7]

It is necessary to read through the quotes several times, and even then it is difficult to believe she really means what she is saying. Butler continues,

> Assuming for the moment the stability of binary sex, it does not follow that the construction of "men" will ac-

crue exclusively to the bodies of males or that "women" will interpret only female bodies. Further, even if the sexes appear to be unproblematically binary in their morphology and constitution (which will become a question) there is no reason to assume that genders ought also to remain as two. The presumption of a binary gender system implicitly retains the belief in a mimetic relations of gender to sex whereby gender mirrors sex or is otherwise restricted by it. When the constructed status of gender is theorized as radically independent of sex, gender itself becomes a free-floating artifice, with the consequence that *man* and *masculine* might just as easily signify a female body as a male one, and *woman* and *feminine* a male body as a female one. [Butler, p. 6]

If the immutable character of sex is contested, perhaps this construct called "sex" is as culturally constructed as gender; indeed, perhaps it was always already gender, with the consequences that the distinction between sex and gender turns out to be no distinction at all. [Butler, p. 7]

In plain English, according to Butler, dividing humanity into two sexes is as arbitrary as assigning people gender roles, and we should not do it.

Reading through Butler's book and the other works in this field, one possible conclusion is that all this postmodernist/ deconstructionist theory is just a front to promote the idea that homosexuality is just as natural as heterosexuality, because "natural" is a hegemonic idea made up by the ruling class to oppress everyone. There is certainly the possibility that if one were to "deconstruct" Butler and other postmodernists, one might find people looking for theories to justify their "lifestyles."

Butler is listed on the board of directors of the International Gay and Lesbian Human Rights Commission. The commission is a U.N. accredited NGO and sponsor of the international petition campaign "Put Sexuality on the Agenda at the World Conference on Women." The campaign was advertised in the NGO forum bulletin September/October 1994. The petition called on member states to recognize "the right to determine one's sexual identity; the right to control one's own body, particularly in establishing intimate relations, and the right to choose if, when and with whom to bear or raise children as fundamental components of the human rights of all women regardless of sexual orientation."

The petition claims these demands are based on article 2 of the Universal Declaration of Human Rights which guarantees protection "without distinction of any kind such as race, color, sex . . . or other status," and that other status would include lesbian status.

While Butler's idea may seem bizarre, this kind of postmodernist/deconstructionist thinking has been influential in shaping feminist thinking and has found its way into the U.N. For example, in the book *Women, Gender, and World Politics*, various writers discuss the relationship of gender to foreign relations and the U.N. In the introduction, Peter Beckman and Francine D'Amico propose the idea that the labels *women* and *men* create fictitious beings and perpetuate inequalities:

> The conception of gender-as-power allows us to take a further step: to suggest that our whole way of *thinking* and *talking* about humans is based on power. The very terms "women" and "men" are a reflection of that power. To label individuals as "women" (or "men") is the exercise of power, for the label creates for human beings a set of expectations about who they are, who they are not, and what range of choice is available to them.

> Gender-as-power argues that women and men are made, not born. They are created by those labels—labels that open some doors and close others. Labeling creates a fictitious being . . . and perpetuates inequalities because the humans carrying one label have more rights and privileges than those carrying the other label. [Peter R. Beckman & Francine D'Amico, *Women, Gender, and World Politics* (Westport, CT: Bergin & Garvey, 1994), p. 7]

Keeping people from labeling men and women would require absolute control of families, education, the media, and private conversation. Inclusive language, however, would just be the tip of the iceberg.

Feminist Fiction

The most radical examples of radical feminism are found not in their speculative discourses, but in their futuristic novels. These novels provide insight into the feminist soul.

In the brave new world Dorothy Bryant created in *The Kin of Ata are Waiting for You*, homosexual and heterosexual relationships are considered equal. Nonpossessive relationships are possible because gender has been eliminated. There are no words for "man," "woman," "he," or "she" [Anne Sisson Runyan "Radical Feminism: Alternative Futures," *Women, Gender, and World Politics*, ed. by Peter R. Beckman & Francine D'Amico (Westport, CT: Bergin & Garvey, 1994), p. 205].

In Ursula Le Guin's *The Dispossessed*, men and women are absolutely equal, sharing in production and reproduction. Heterosexuality and homosexual relationships are equal, and there are no possessive pronouns, no marriage [Runyan, p. 205].

In the utopian feminist community created by Marge Piercy in *Woman on the Edge of Time*, not only has gender been eliminated, but biological sex has been rendered ambiguous. Babies are created in test tubes, and each baby has three "comothers," male and female, all of whom are treated with hormones so that they can breastfeed. People are called "per" rather than "he" or "she" and have sexual relationships with males and females [Anne Sisson, p. 206]. One of Piercy's characters explains why this was necessary:

> It was part of women's long revolution. When we were breaking all the old hierarchies. Finally, there was one thing we had to give up too, the only power we ever had, in return for no more power for anyone. The original production: the power of birth. Cause as long as we were biologically enchained we'd never been equal. And males never would be humanized to be loving and tender. So we all became mothers. Every child has three. To break the nuclear bonding. [Marge Piercy, *Woman on the Edge of Time* (New York, Random House, 1971), p. 105, quoted by Runyan, p. 207]

The attitude toward mothering in these novels is indicative of the direction of radical feminist thinking. The writers see mothering as repressive only when women do it. If it is done by men or the community, it is liberating [Runyan, p. 207]. While these particular feminist novelists come back to the same theme—men must be changed; they must adopt caring nonhierarchical, noncompetitive attitudes—their view is not shared by the lesbian and matriarchal separatist novelists. Holding out no hope for this transformation of men, separatists write of women who have separated from men in order to save themselves and the world.

The New Revolution

For those who think that Marxism died with the fall of the Berlin Wall, the radical and gender feminists' reliance on Marxist analysis may seem strange. In fact, Marxist analysis is flourishing on American campuses. When I inquired of a professor at Mt. Holyoke College why Marxism was so appealing to the academic Left, he replied that atheists need something to believe in. Marxism provides that something. It offers a comprehensive world view and a cause for which to fight. And, Marxism offers the academic elite power; it is their opportunity to become the masters of the revolution.

While radical and gender feminists begin with Marxist analysis, they have moved in an entirely different direction from the economic and political Marxists. They aren't working for a Communist revolution, but a cultural revolution. They want to pull down the family, not the state. Their enemies aren't the bourgeois capitalists, but "Puritans," "fundamentalists," "the Religious Right," and "the Holy See."

These Neo-Marxists are interested in "progressive" politics, politically correct programs, multiculturalism, and diversity. They promote victimology—the creation of new classes of "oppressed." While Neo-Marxists frequently masquerade as political liberals, they do not share the liberal commitment to free speech and equal rights. They claim to be the defenders of justice and fairness, but their style of justice and fairness applies only to the "oppressed." Furthermore, when these Neo-Marxists get into positions of power, they rarely respect the rights of those who disagree with them.

Numerous voices have been raised against the totalitarian spirit of the politically correct, Neo-Marxist Left, but none more eloquent than that of David Horowitz, who, as editor of *Ramparts* magazine, was once among their shining lights. Horowitz recognized that, while the Marxist Left talks about liberation and freedom, they are committed to a destructive utopian idea. In *Destructive Generation: Second Thoughts about the '60s,* he writes:

> Compassion is not what motivates the Left, which is oblivious to the human suffering its generations have caused. What motivates the Left is the totalitarian Idea: the Idea that is more important than reality itself. What motivates the Left is the Idea of the future in which everything is changed, everything *transcended.* The future in which the present is already *annihilated;* in which its reality no longer exists.
>
> What motivates the Left is an Idea whose true consciousness is this: *Everything human is alien.* Because everything that is flesh-and-blood humanity is only the disposable past. This is the consciousness that makes mass murderers of well-intentioned humanists and earnest progressives. [David Horowitz and Peter Collier, *Destructive Generation: Second Thoughts about the '60s* (New York: Summit Books, 1989), p. 288]

Profamily advocates have struggled in vain to show the feminists and their allies the disasters their policies have caused, pointing to the urban wastelands, the fatherless children, the aborted millions, the toll of sexually transmitted diseases, the deserted and divorced women. What the profamily advocates do not understand, however, is that feminists know the cost and accept it as the inevitable price of revolution. They are convinced that the future will be so wonderful that any suffering needed to achieve their ends will have been justified.

Ten

Division of Labor

The most obvious effect of the Marx/Engels/Firestone influence is the demonizing of "patriarchy" as the great evil. *Patriarchal* has become an all-purpose curse word. It is interesting that many people have accepted that patriarchy is evil without considering the ideological roots of this accusation.

Marxist feminist Heidi Hartman defines patriarchy as

> men's control over women's labor power. That control is maintained by excluding women from access to necessary economically productive resources and by restricting women's sexuality. Men exercise their control in receiving personal service work from women, in not having to do housework or rear children, in having access to women's bodies for sex, and in feeling powerful and being powerful. [Heidi Hartman, "The Unhappy Marriage of Marxism and Feminism," *Women and Revolution*, ed. by Lydia Sargent (Boston: South End Press, 1981), p. 18]

According to Hartman, the "elements of patriarchy as we *currently* experience them are: heterosexual marriage (and consequent homophobia), female childrearing and housework, women's economic dependence on men (enforced by arrangements in the labor market), the state, and numerous institutions based on social relations among men—clubs, sports, unions, professions, universities, churches, corporations and armies."

The institution in which men "have access to women's bodies for sex," "receive personal service work from women," and don't have "to do housework or rear children" is, of course, the one-income/two-parent family. Many women would contend that the division of labor between men and women in the one-income/two-parent family is just and serves their interests as much as their husbands'. But, for the radical, Marxist, and socialist feminists, the one-income/two-parent family is a patriarchal evil that must be destroyed by a radical change in the relationship between men and women.

While radical feminists see patriarchy as the great evil, patriarchy could also be seen as men accepting responsibility for their wives and children. A society which is suffering from an epidemic of father-absent families ought to consider whether the war on "patriarchy" has benefited women. Women who want to make motherhood their primary vocation need men who are willing to commit to fatherhood and a society where men take responsibility for protecting and providing for women and children.

For the radical feminists, it is not just that the one-income/two-parent family oppresses women. They see the family as the cause of all other forms of oppression and the foundation of "patriarchal, hierarchical, sexist, racist, homophobic society." It is not enough for them that some women reject the patriarchal relationships. They believe that as long as some women choose this form of association, all women are threatened.

According to Nancy Chodorow, in the father-working/mother-at-home family, the child is psychologically conditioned to believe that the two sexes are different. Girls identify with their mothers, and boys realize that they are not going to grow up and be mothers. According to Chodorow, the differences between men and women are created (socially constructed) by these early experiences. Once the concept of two different sexes is ingrained in the child's mind, the child will see other "class" divisions, and the evil of class thinking will have been transmitted to another generation.

Thus, in the radical feminist world view, motherhood is the problem, specifically women as primary caregivers to young children. How can this be overcome? For Chodorow, it is not enough to get all women into the workforce and all children into daycare because day-care workers are predominantly female. Men must accept 50 percent of the care for children:

> If our goal is to overcome the sexual division of labor in which women mother, we need to understand the mechanisms which reproduce it in the first place. My account points precisely to where intervention should take place. Any strategy for change whose goal includes liberation from the constraints of an unequal social organization of gender must take account of the need for a fundamental reorganization of parenting, so that primary parenting is shared between men and women. [Nancy Chodorow, *The Reproduction of Mothering* (Berkeley: University of California Press, 1978), p. 215]

Chodorow's analysis has received widespread support among feminists. For them, it pinpointed the problem: Women care for children. It pointed to the solution: Make men care for children. It explained why women hadn't embraced the revolution: They were brainwashed because they we.e raised by mothers. And, it explained how men had kept control of everything: They were raised not to mother.

Gender

By combining these theories, the feminists were able to create an ideology which explained everything to their satisfaction. Now, they needed a plan. They could agree with Firestone that men are the primordial oppressor class, women the first and most oppressed class, and that the only answer is total abolition of the sex class system, but how does one create a classless society when class differences are rooted in biology? You can't strip away manhood the way you can take away private property. The feminists couldn't, as their Bolshevik brothers had done, take the oppressor class out and shoot them or ship all men off to Siberia, although occasionally reading radical feminist and lesbian separatist literature, one gets the feeling that they wish they could. On the bus to the Non-Governmental Organization Forum during the conference on women in Beijing, feminists were overheard musing about how wonderful it would be when there were all-women cities and only girl babies. Nevertheless, most feminists recognize the impracticability of promoting a world without men. There would have to be another means of removing the oppression of the class "men" over the class "women."

Feminist theorists solved this problem by inventing a new meaning for *gender*. The redefinition of *gender* allowed them to claim that they accepted biological "sex" differences and were only rejecting social and cultural "gender" roles. Gender became the focus of the feminist revolution. An INSTRAW booklet explains the new definition of *gender*:

> What is gender? Gender is a concept that refers to a system of roles and relationships between women and men that are determined not by biology but the social, political, and economic context. One's biological sex is a natural *given;* gender is constructed. . . . gender can be seen as the ". . . *process by which individuals who are born into biological categories of male or female become the social categories of women and men through the acquisition of locally defined attributes of masculinity and femininity.*" ["Gender Concepts in Development Planning: Basic Approach" (INSTRAW, 1995), p. 11]

Using "gender analysis," feminists avoided being perceived as attacking biology. They could admit that sex differences were natural and fixed, but insist that all the important differences between men and women were gender differences. And, artificial gender differences can be transformed.

Gender analysis is not a scientific study of the relative influence of biology and culture in the creation of the differences between men and women. Indeed, gender feminists vigorously oppose serious research into biological differences between men and women. The Gender Agenda is predicated on the unproved assumption that masculinity, femininity, manhood, womanhood, motherhood, fatherhood, and heterosexuality are artificial, arbitrary, culturally created "gender roles."

The goal is statistical equality between men and women in all activities and achievements. The major obstacle to statistical equality is mothering—the vocation of women as primary caregivers for children. If the majority of women or even a significant percentage of women choose mothering as their primary vocation, then statistical equality becomes statistically impossible, since the number of women available for work outside the home is substantially reduced. Thus, the major thrust of "gender perspective" is the deconstruction of mothering as the unique vocation of women.

Nothing more clearly illustrates the real nature of the gender perspective than the following quote from the INSTRAW booklet: "Nothing in the fact that women bear children implies that they exclusively should care for them throughout childhood" [Maureen Mackintosh, "Gender and Economics" quoted in *Gender Concepts*, p. 18].

According to this view, women's desire to mother—that is to be intimately concerned with the day to day care of their children, particularly their newborns—is regarded as something imposed upon them by a patriarchal society.

It is not surprising that Supreme Court Justice Ruth Bader Ginsburg, in a speech in New York, called motherly love a myth: "Motherly love ain't all it has been cracked up to be. To some extent, it's a myth that men have created to make women think that they do this job to perfection" [Joan Biskupic, "Ruth Bader Ginsburg: Feminist Justice," *Washington Post* reprinted in *Providence Journal*, 20 July 1996, p. 13 ("Hers" section)].

Gender Justice

The feminists had solved their problem—radical feminism was transformed into the "gender perspective." In her book, *Justice, Gender, and the Family*, feminist writer Susan Okin lays out how the gender perspective can be implemented; and it all sounds very reasonable, very compassionate, very just:

> A just future would be one without gender. In its social structures and practices, one's sex would have no more relevance than one's eye color or the length of one's toes. No assumptions would be made about "male" and "female" roles; childbearing would be so conceptually separated from child rearing and other family responsibilities

that it would be cause for surprise, and no little concern, if men and women were not equally responsible for domestic life or if children were to spend much more time with one parent than the other. It would be a future in which men and women participated in more or less equal numbers in every sphere of life, from infant care to different kinds of paid work to high-level politics. [Susan Okin, *Justice, Gender, and the Family* (New York: Basic Books, 1989), p. 170]

Okin insists that "shared child rearing is a prerequisite of justice between the sexes" because female childrearing:

(1) "is immensely time-consuming, and prevents those who do it single-handedly from the pursuit of many other social goods, such as education, earnings, or political office,"

(2) is the cause of "sex stereotyping in children" [Okin, fn.p. 116].

Okin recognizes that many women find child care pleasurable. However, since female childrearing renders women economically vulnerable, it must be eliminated. According to Okin, "Because asymmetric vulnerabilities create social obligations, which may fail to be fulfilled, and because they open up opportunities for exploitation . . . they are morally unacceptable and should be minimized" [Okin, p. 136].

It is certainly true that pregnancy and childrearing make women vulnerable. Precisely for this reason societies have offered various forms of protection to women. These protections have been predicated on the differences between the sexes, and it is these very protections that feminists have condemned as restricting women. Unwilling to acknowledge women's need for special protection, the only solution Okin can accept is one which denies the differences between the sexes. She insists that "any just and fair solution to the urgent problem of women's and children's vulnerability must encourage and facilitate the equal sharing by men and women of paid and unpaid work, of productive and reproductive labor. We must work toward a future in which all will be likely to choose this mode of life" [Okin, p. 170].

The last sentence is crucial. While the radical feminists speak of liberation and choice, they do not extend that freedom to women who choose to make mothering their primary vocation. Okin wants a world where every woman will be forced to work full-time.

These daughters of Marx may have rejected their ideological father's economic agenda, but they have inherited his totalitarian soul. The liberation they promote is not a personal freedom, but a single-party state where some women decide what is best for all women. The Soviet system controlled the political and economic structures; the feminists want control of intimate and family relationships.

From Theory to Practice

All this theory may seem very far from the reality of ordinary women, but it is closely related to what is happening at the U.N. Feminist theory explains why the INSTRAW, the U.N. agency in charge of research on women, isn't interested in helping women solve their real problems. The INSTRAW booklet discourages such help since it might keep them in their current positions as wives and mothers: "Most development work dealing with women focuses on women's condition, emphasizing such immediate needs as access to credit, basic services, housing and attention to their responsibilities as mothers. . . . Exclusive attention to improvements in women's condition can reinforce patterns that perpetuate inequalities" [*Gender Concepts*, p. 27].

INSTRAW recognizes that women need help in their work in the home, but doesn't want to give women that help because it might keep them at home: "Women's practical needs are generally derived from existing gender roles assigned to them by traditional patterns of division of labour. . . . Satisfying practical needs alone reproduces divisions of labour and power that maintain the status quo" [*Gender Concepts*, p. 27].

Instead, INSTRAW supports programs which will force women into the workforce. All this is based on gender feminist theory. The booklet contrasts women's needs with women's "strategic interests":

Strategic interests, in contrast, challenge existing gender roles and stereotypes, based on the premise that women are in a subordinate position to men as the consequence of social and institutional discrimination against them. . . . Strategic gender interests seek such objectives as political equality between women and men, elimination of institutionalized forms of discrimination against women, abolition of the sexual division of labour, freedom of reproductive choice, and prevention of violence against women. [*Gender Concepts*, p. 28]

There is no evidence that INSTRAW asked the poor women of the world if they wanted their gender roles changed or preferred more practical help. The INSTRAW booklet follows the totalitarian spirit of feminism revealed by Simone de Beauvoir, who told Betty Friedan: "No woman should be authorized to stay at home to raise her children. . . . Women should not have that choice, precisely because if there is such a choice too many women will make that one" [quoted by Christina Hoff Sommers, *Who Stole Feminism?* (New York: Simon and Schuster, 1994), p. 256].

According to Alison Jagger, "If individual desires and interests are socially constituted . . . people may be mistaken about truth, morality or even their own interests" [quoted by Sommers, p. 258]. In other words, ordinary women should not be allowed to decide what they want because they have all been socially conditioned to want the wrong things. All this demeans women, as Christina Hoff Sommers, an outspoken critic of gender feminism, points out: "In the end, the gender feminist is always forced to show her disappointment and annoyance with the women found in the camp of the enemy. Misandry moves on to misogyny" [Sommers, p. 256].

Profamily advocates oppose the gender perspective not because they are against women's progress, but because they are for women. Should the feminist future ever arrive, it won't be more just, but less free and less human.

Eleven

Redefining Equality

The gender feminists, realizing they could not sell a direct attack on mothering and the family or postmodernist deconstructionism to the general public, focused on redefining equality. Everyone believes in equality. It is a great word. It brings to mind that noble statement of human aspiration—the U.S. Declaration of Independence: "We hold these truths to be self-evident—that all men are created equal; that they are endowed by their Creator with certain inalienable rights."

What could be more clever than to take that noble aspiration and twist it to mean something that was never intended—statistically equal rates of participation, achievement, and rewards—distorting the democratic ideal of equal dignity, equal humanity, and equal rights into a demand for a Neo-Marxist classless society?

What is amazing is that this radical change in meaning has gone largely unreported and undebated.

There can be no question that the writers of the draft platform for Beijing intended to redefine equality. An even cursory reading of the platform reveals that the "full and equal participation of women" called for requires participation in statistically equal numbers—fifty/fifty. In paragraph 192 [190] of the section "Women in power and decision-making," governments are called on to do the following:

[C]ommit themselves to establishing the *goal of gender balance* in governmental bodies and committees, as well as in pubic administrative entities and in the judiciary, including, inter alia setting *specific targets* and implementing measures to substantially increase the number of women with a view to *achieving equal representation* of women and men, if necessary through positive action, in all governmental and public administration positions . . . Take *measures*, including where appropriate, in electoral systems that encourage political parties to integrate women in elective and non-elective public positions in the *same proportion* and levels as men . . . Review the *differential impact* of electoral systems on the political representations of women in elected bodies and consider, where appropriate, the adjustment or reform of those systems . . . Monitor and evaluate progress on the representation of women. (emphasis added)

It is amazing how many ways one can call for quotas without using the word.

Fifty/fifty by 2005

Fifty/fifty by 2005 was one of the goals set by WEDO. The Council of Europe meeting also strongly supported "quotas or parity" for women. The ideological justification for this demand is laid out in a book edited by Mim Kelber, with an introduction coauthored by Bella Abzug, *Women and Government: New Ways to Political Power*. The book contains Professor Elisabeth Sledziewski's argument that real democracy is not possible without "gender" quotas: "Only the introduction of participation quotas imposing equal representation of the sexes in all decision-making authorities can make women's participation in the *polis* effective and irreversible" [Mim Kelber, *Women and Government: New Ways to Political Power* (Westport, CT: Praeger, 1994), p. 33].

Dr. Sledziewski does not see quotas as a temporary measure:

Measures put forward to foster the involvement of women in the political life must not be presented, as they too often are, as conjunctural arrangement for the achievement of results on an ad hoc basis and devoid of any doctrinal justification. This approach could not fail to confirm the unfair suspicions voiced in connection with quotas and suggest that the involvement of women in politics can only be enforced by unlawful means. On the contrary, it is necessary to affirm that these provisions are envisaged in the very name of the principle of equality. [Kelber, p. 33]

Democracy would be redefined:

The advent of democracy based on equal representation will mean not only a turning point in relations between men and women and consequently in the social being of the human race, but also a turning point in the democratic construction process. Equal participation by female citizens in the affairs of the *polis* will henceforth be considered a *sine qua non* for the completion of democracy. A democracy without women will no longer be seen as an imperfect democracy but as no democracy at all. [Kelber, p. 33]

Dr. Sledziewski admits, however, that this is a rejection of the modern ideal of European democracy and the rights of the individual.

When this book and the WEDO Global Strategies report were reviewed in an article in *Catholic World Report*, Mim Kelber, in a letter to the editor, expressed her indignation that the article had referred to fifty/fifty by 2005 as a call for quotas and gender police:

Your February 1995 issue contains misrepresentations and faulty alleged quotations from a book *Women and Government New Ways to Political Power* of which I was the editor and chief writer. The book also included an introduction that I wrote with Bella Abzug and that sets out our views on "quotas" a term used pejoratively in your article.

In chapter 1 on "What American Woman Can Do to Win Equality" I proposed a constitutional amendment that would double the size of the US Senate to 200 members with two men and two women elected from each state by both male and female voters. . . . The use of numerical goals is a mechanism recognized in many political parties as a way to work toward achievement of equal participation by women and men in governance.

I strongly support equal opportunity and affirmative action programs to overcome past and continuing employment discrimination against women and minorities, but I have never advocated a strict 50-50 quota for every job category in the private sector. What you call "gender police," I call the staff of the Equal Employment Opportunity Commission.

Mim Kelber, Brooklyn NY

To which the editor of *Catholic World Report*, Phil Lawler, replied, "If a 'numerical goal' is not a quota and if a legislature whose seats are open only to members of the appropriate sex is not an example of enforced gender equality, then we stand corrected" [April 1995].

While Kelber has not specifically argued for fifty/fifty in every job category in the private sector, there is discussion of the lack of statistical equality in the private sector. In addition, the WEDO Global Strategies report calls for 50 percent women in key positions by 2005 in "private corporations and financial institutions, trade unions, international financial institutions."

This same demand for fifty/fifty was part of the declaration issued by a conference of parliamentarians held in Tokyo in September 1996. The parliamentarians, many of them on their way to Beijing, called on governments to "assure that, by the year 2005, women constitute at least 50% of the membership of all government bodies, including elected and appointed positions at international, national and local levels" [Jack Freeman, "Global Lawmakers, in Tokyo, Say That Population Must Be Concern," *Earth Times* (5 September 1995)].

Of course, not everyone signed on to fifty/fifty quotas. Mahbub ul Haq, former finance minister of Pakistan and chief architect of UNDP's annual Human Development Reports, questioned the wisdom of such a goal, even though his country has a woman prime minister:

But how can we say that, in every society and every culture, women must have exactly 50% of the jobs or 50% of parliamentary seats, or 50% of heads of multi-national—kicking and screaming, whether they like it or not? The most important point is that free and equal choices must exist for societies, but they cannot be dictated for societies, . . . by some misconceived universal models. ["Let Beijing Develop meaningful gender equality," *Earth Times*, 14 September 1995, p. 6]

The promoters of fifty/fifty by 2005 want to pretend that they are only trying to achieve the equality promised in the U.N.'s Universal Declaration of Human Rights, but this is not the case. In the first article of the declaration, the word *equality* is used in the classic sense: "All human beings are born free and equal in dignity and rights."

Nowhere does the declaration require governments to enforce statistically equal participation.

Gender Disaggregated Statistics

The Beijing platform repeatedly calls for "gender disaggregated statistics." If equality is measurable, then someone must do the measuring so that the feminists can prove "inequalities." The existence of "inequalities" in participation, achievement, or rewards is then taken as proof of discrimination, not evidence that men and women are different. Those who accept the differences between men and women expect different rates of participation. They see no reason why equal rights and opportunity should result in statistically equal participation.

The immediate goal of gender feminists is to create a climate of opinion where equality is defined not as equal rights and opportunities, but as statistically equal participation, achievement, and rewards. Most people laugh at the idea of a constitutional amendment to make the Senate fifty/fifty; however, they do not recognize that the feminist complaint that only 10 percent of the Congress is made up of women is based on the same false premise.

Feminists routinely use statistical inequalities between men and women as proof of discrimination. They complained that women only made fifty-nine cents for every dollar men made.

When it rose to seventy-two cents for every dollar, they still complained, even though the difference in aggregate wages reflects not discrimination but women's decisions to take time off for their families. The feminist complaint that a "glass ceiling" keeps women from high-level jobs is based on statistical evidence. Their complaint that SATs discriminate against women is based on statistical differences in scores. There may or may not have been actual discrimination, but they don't even try to make that case. For them, quoting the statistics is sufficient proof.

Once the feminists have convinced their audience that equality has been denied, they then demand quotas or affirmative action as remedies.

The promoters of statistical equality do not present evidence that men and women wish to participate in every occupational category in statistically equal numbers because there is none. For the feminists, the lack of desire for statistical equality merely proves that women have been socialized by "gender stereotyping."

Therefore, in addition to quotas, the feminists demand removal of "stereotypes" and "traditional images" from educational materials and media presentations. In order to achieve equality of desire and interest, school textbooks, cartoons, soap operas, advertisements, and dramas would show men and women employed in equal numbers as soldiers, scientists, firemen, and truck drivers, even when this has no relation to reality; activities in which only men participate would be categorized as evil, oppressive, and discriminatory; women would never be shown as full-time mothers and homemakers, unless they were portrayed as victims of battering, sociopathy, or have religious fanatics as husbands.

Thus, the redefinition of equality requires an entire gender enforcement bureaucracy, with gatherers of gender disaggregated statistics, gender analysis experts, gender sensitivity trainers, and equal opportunity commissioners. This would supply permanent employment for graduates of women's studies programs and give feminists virtual control over every institution of society. Much of this is already in the process of being implemented in government, education, and business.

Opponents of affirmative action and quotas charge that these stigmatize the targeted groups as people who lack the ability to compete on an equal playing field. The qualifications of all members of the targeted group, even those who could succeed without quotas, come under suspicion. Once affirmative action and quotas become the rule, there is no way for the targeted groups to prove their ability. Justice Clarence Thomas, who has been accused of not supporting the affirmative action programs from which he benefited, has pointed out that affirmative action steals the satisfaction of achievement.

Real justice involves the elimination of unjust discrimination, not an attack on natural differences and personal preferences. A campaign to eradicate differences attacks personal freedom.

There is no way to judge the percentage of women who should be employed in any particular field because there is no way to judge how many women are interested in such employment. Girls should not be discouraged from pursuing a career in a "nontraditional" field; neither should they be forced to do so. Textbooks and media presentations of occupations should accurately reflect the actual male/female ratio in a particular field. Knowing that a particular field has been predominantly or even exclusively male has not discouraged women from seeking employment in that field. Indeed, experience suggests that some women enjoy the challenge of proving themselves in a male-dominated field. So long as no artificial barriers (qualifications which are not job-related) exist, no specific numerical quota should be set and no particular statistical ratio between men and women expected.

When artificial barriers to women's participation in various fields are eliminated, there will be changes in participation rates, as a study in *Ms.* magazine showed. Comparing the percentage of women eighteen to sixty-five employed in selected professions in 1970 and 1990, *Ms.* reported that the number of women employed in certain fields had risen substantially.

Women employed as bartenders increased from 26 percent to 52 percent, bus drivers from 32 percent to 50 percent, lawyers and judges from 6 percent to 26 percent. In other fields, however, such as the armed forces, auto mechanics, librarians, nurses, pilots, secretaries, and teachers, the percentage remained the same [Applied Social Research program, Queens College, CUNY, quoted in *Ms.* (November/December 1995), p. 40].

Equality of opportunity and the elimination of arbitrary discrimination against women will change the distribution of women and men in the workforce, but there is no reason to assume that it will ever result in a fifty/fifty split in every job category, nor given the natural differences between men and women, is there any reason why it should. Indeed, the elimination of artificial barriers may reveal that the so-called stereotypes reflected the real differences in women's and men's interests and talents.

Reverse Discrimination

Mandating quotas for women/men in elected office doesn't create instant justice, but a different injustice. It would give potential women candidates an unfair advantage, since women do not seek political office in numbers equal to men. There are a number of reasons for this: 1) In every country a significant portion of the women, including the brightest and most talented choose to make motherhood their primary vocation and do not choose to work outside the home or to run for public office; 2) Many women who are talented and motivated choose to support their husbands' political careers. In the U.S. Elizabeth Dole, Marilyn Quail, and Hillary Clinton are prime examples of women who could have equaled their husbands, but chose not to.

Mandating fifty/fifty denies women the freedom to vote for the candidates of their choice. There is no evidence that all women feel their interests are better represented by women. Today, women make up over 50 percent of the electorate in most countries. They are perfectly free to vote for women, to organize women's parties, and to demand the nomination of women candidates. Women could elect 100 percent women if they wanted to.

The promoters of the Gender Agenda may talk about women as decision makers, but they don't like the decisions that women make.

Twelve

The War on Motherhood

If fifty/fifty is the goal, what is the obstacle? Mothers; in particular, every woman who makes motherhood her primary vocation, whether or not she works outside the home. There is no way that fifty/fifty can be achieved if a substantial portion of women choose not to work full-time.

The Beijing draft document referred to motherhood negatively and did not contain a single program for women who are full-time mothers and homemakers. This was not an oversight.

The platform accurately reflects the feminist attitude to the family and motherhood. Feminist Jane Flax compiled a "survey of contemporary feminist thought on the family." She notes that the major feminist writers, Betty Friedan, Kate Millett, Shulamith Firestone, Juliet Mitchell, Gayle Rubin, Dorothy Dinnerstein, and Nancy Chodorow, all see the family and, in particular, mothering, as the source of women's oppression [J. Flax, "The Family in Contemporary Feminist Thought: A Critical Review," *The Family in Political Thought* (Amherst, MA: University of Massachusetts Press, 1982), quoted by Letty Cotten Pogrebin, *Family Politics* (NY: McGraw-Hill, 1983), pp. 22-24].

According to feminist theory, mothering causes class thinking, and classes are the cause of all evil. The only way to save the world is to eliminate mothering. The feminist theorists offer various solutions for the problem: "better jobs and education so that women can 'have it all' ''; "a cultural revolution" and "altered social consciousness"; "test tube babies" and diffusing "childrearing responsibility among many households"; "full involvement of fathers in child care" [Pogrebin, p. 22-24].

It should be pointed out that while radical and gender feminists believe that the role of mother and wife is stultifying, if they have children, they love them, and there is no evidence that feminists are bad mothers. Bella Abzug is a proud mother and grandmother. But, this does not prevent her and other feminists from viewing mothering as a political problem.

While radical and gender feminists oppose the traditional family, they recognize the word *family* cannot simply be junked. Like equality, they want the family redefined. Christine Riddiough suggested using gay/lesbian culture as a means of redefining the family.

According to feminist Ellen Herman, feminists don't want to eliminate families, but to redesign them:

> (Young feminists) . . . wanted the freedom to design their present and future families in myriad ways, without penalty: to love women or men, to have sex with one person at a time or several, to live with or without children, to participate in parenting without necessarily participating in reproduction. Only when they could invent families of all kinds—without fear of ridicule or self-loathing—could women hope to attain genuine individuality, rather than categorization as captive members of a sex/gender class. [Ellen Herman, "Still Married After All These Years," *Sojourner: The Women's Forum* (September 1990), p. 14s]

Nancy Chodorow calls for shared parenting to overcome the oppression of "the sexual division of labor in which women mother." The Beijing platform incorporates the theme, referring repeatedly to "shared family responsibility." Paragraph 181(d) specifically calls on governments to "[c]hange attitudes that reinforce the division of labour based on gender in order to promote the concept of shared family responsibility for work in the home, particularly in relation to children and elder care."

For feminists, changing the division of labor in the family is key to their revolution. The classless society requires abolition of the freedom of couples to decide for themselves how to organize their families.

Profamily advocates do not believe that every mother must stay at home or that fathers should not be involved with their children or help with housework. They believe that individual couples have the right to divide the work of the family as they think best. If both husband and wife want to share equally in work outside and inside the home, they should be free to do so. But, if they want to divide the work differently, if the mother wants to stay home with her children, the government should not interfere or penalize that decision.

The promotion of "shared family responsibility" is not about fairness to women, but part of the strategy to promote statistical equality. According to Vigdís Finnbogadóttir, the president of Iceland and an active advocate of the gender perspective,

> As long as the private sphere remains largely women's concern, they will be much less available than men for positions of responsibility in economic and political life.

> Among the strategies, mention might be made of the generalisation of parental leave, shared between mothers and fathers, greater availability of childcare facilities, care for the old and encouragement for men to participate in housework. [Council of Europe, *Equality or Democracy: Utopia or Challenge?, Reports from Discussion Groups* (Palais d'Europe, Strasbourg, 9-11 February 1995), p. 38]

Several Nordic nations have tried to find ways to force men to take parental leave. To agree that fathers should take an active part in the raising of their children, however, does not mean that fathering is the same as mothering. Children may need different things from their fathers than from their mothers. The promoters of the Gender Agenda aren't concerned about the psychological needs of children, but in transforming the relationship between men and women.

Finnbogadóttir's speech reveals that the real enemy of the Gender Agenda is not men, but women—women who want to make motherhood their primary vocation. The promoters of the Gender Agenda understand that if women choose motherhood in significant numbers, they will not be available to achieve statistical equality. Even the most ardent advocates of the Gender Agenda do not pretend that they can induce a significant number of men to make full-time childcare their primary vocation.

Fifty/fifty by 2005 requires zero full-time mothers, and the Beijing platform is the blueprint for reaching that goal.

Economic Effects

One of the arguments made for all women in the workforce is that in order to develop economically, societies need to take advantage of the talents of all citizens. Full-time mothers find this kind of argument insulting. The clear implication is that women who work within the home are wasting their talents and education. Making a human being is the most important work in society, and devoting one's talents and energies to this task should be considered as productive as working in a factory or office.

New research on the brain reveals that the crucial time for the development of language, emotional stability, and reasoning ability occurs from birth to five years. A child who does not receive the proper input during this crucial period is forever handicapped. The child's brain needs precisely the kind of one-on-one interaction that a mother provides. It is interesting that an article in *Newsweek* discussing the discoveries that led to this conclusion makes almost no mention of mothers as the suppliers of this interaction. Instead, it discusses the need for "intensive early education in a day-center from 4 months" [Sharon Begley, "Your Child's Brain," *Newsweek*, 19 February 1996, p. 61].

While well-paid mother substitutes could supply the input needed for brain development, the cost would be prohibitive. A woman who works at a low-paying job can't afford to pay a skilled professional to do her mothering. Those who want all women in the workforce recognize this and call for government-subsidized day care, but where would the subsidies come from? Taxes on families—taxes which force more mothers into the workforce.

Babies come with committed day-care providers who are willing and able to supply the one-on-one interaction needed for brain development—mothers. Mothers don't need a master's degree in education to learn how to talk baby-talk to babies. Furthermore, babies already have a fully equipped day-care center right at home. And, babies are better off if they are not exposed to sick children, particularly since frequent ear infections in infancy are now blamed for later language problems.

Feminists complain that women are made to feel guilty when they put their children in day care, and this is probably because most women know that even the best day care is a second-rate imitation of a home and mother. And, very few working mothers can afford the best.

Profamily lobbyists argue that instead of subsidies for day-care and child-care tax credits for working mothers, there should be tax credits for all children, or better, significantly lower taxes on all families, so that mothers aren't forced into the workforce.

This solution would not be acceptable to radical and gender feminists, since their version of empowerment requires that all women be employed in paid work and be economically autonomous. The definition of empowerment as economic independence ignores the reality of women's lives. Pregnancy, childbirth, and motherhood affect women's workplace participation. When a woman is not employed because of family responsibilities, she depends on her husband and the father of her children for economic support. This "economic dependence" empowers women to make the choice of motherhood. The emphasis on paid work ignores the desires of women. The profamily position supports the woman's right to decide for herself whether she will work full-time, be a full-time mother, or choose part-time work so she can devote her energies to her family.

Forcing all women into the workforce has other economic effects. It increases the supply of workers, thereby lowering the demand and lowering wages. If men are unable to support their families on a single paycheck, more women are forced into the workforce, setting off a downward spiral. When women in poor countries are recruited into the workforce for extremely low wages, jobs move to these countries, and the ability of men to support their families deteriorates further.

When both parents are forced to work, the stresses on the family increase. School-age children receive less supervision. This increases the need for various kinds of government programs and the taxes to pay for them.

One way families cope with these stresses is by limiting their families to one or two children. While most people believe that the world is suffering from an uncontrolled population explosion, the major economic problem in the next century will be the birth dearth. An aging population dependent on expensive government health and retirement programs will demand increased subsidies from a shrinking pool of workers. This further increases the tax burden.

Feminists insist that women who work outside the home gain economic autonomy, but if the majority of a woman's salary is eaten up by higher taxes, day care, and the cost of additional services, a woman may be only marginally better off. Some women argue that a woman at home has true autonomy. She is her own boss, running her house, organizing her time, and making her own decisions. Very often, she manages the family income and makes most of the spending decisions.

Feminists are very concerned with who makes decisions. They want fifty/fifty quotas on all decision-making positions, particularly high-level decision making. But, most women do not feel more liberated if the bureaucrat or politician making the decisions that influence their lives is a woman. What they want is to make their own decisions, or to have decisions made at the lowest level of government where the voices of ordinary women can be heard.

The big government solutions envisioned in the Beijing platform take decision making away from the local level and invest power in bureaucracies. Power is taken from the people and given to the government. Mandating quotas on bureaucracies will not return power to ordinary women.

Traditional Roles

Of all the paragraphs in the Beijing Platform, the one that profamily women found the most offensive was the gratuitous insult in paragraph 77, which condemned school curriculum for showing men and women in "traditional female and male roles." The paragraph says that "traditional female and male roles . . . deny women opportunities for full and equal partnership in society."

Profamily women reject the idea that full-time mothers are second-class citizens trapped into subordinate and subservient roles, waiting to be freed by full-time employment so that society can take advantage of their talents. "We have not been denied opportunities," one of the profamily women pointed out. "These feminists seem to think that we don't leave the house. We are here in Beijing."

Typical of the profamily women in Beijing was Cecilia Royals, mother of eight, who founded the National Institute of Womanhood and organized the Well-being of Women Caucus. Cecilia cannot be classed among the rich and privileged. Her husband is a teacher in a private school. Three of her children have serious birth defects. Her activism does not detract from her commitment to family, precisely because she doesn't also have to work outside the home. Visitors to the Royals' small but neat home just outside Washington feel as though they have stepped into a scene from a Louisa May Alcott novel. The children help with dinner, and the meal is followed by a piano recital and poetry reading.

Karen McNeil, a lovely wife and mother from Memphis, has taken an active part in the life of her community and church, organizing a group which helps pregnant women find ways to have their babies and supporting the battle against sexually oriented businesses. When she heard about the Beijing conference, she felt called to attend. She raised the money by speaking to groups in Memphis. Karen, a real steel magnolia, had been concerned about the risks of going to China, but when the time came to take a stand, Karen joined five other American women who stood up with a banner in silent protest to the U.S. failure to support families and life. As a result, she and the rest of the women were taken into custody. Their credentials were confiscated, and they were placed under house arrest in the Catic Hotel. It is interesting to note that when lesbian activists staged a noisy protest at the conference, they were neither arrested nor penalized.

Full-time motherhood doesn't mean that a woman has no time for anything else. Besides homeschooling two of her four children, Genevieve Kineke edits *Hearth* magazine from her family room. She is currently developing a home page on the World Wide Web for the Alliance of Catholic Women. She prepared lobbying materials for the Cairo and Beijing conferences which included the following Motherhood Manifesto, which was circulated to delegates at the PrepCom:

The Motherhood Manifesto

• Every woman who believes her place is in the home should be able to be there.

• Women shall not be forced to work outside the home, whether by law, economics, or social pressure. Mothers who do work outside the home shall have sufficient leave to recover from childbirth, nurse their babies, and care for sick family members.

• Governments should protect the economic security of women who work within the home.

• Everything possible should be done to protect a woman's potential ability to bear children.

• No woman should be forced, coerced, paid, or bribed to surrender or endanger her reproductive potential through sterilization, contraception, abortion, or sexual or reproductive servitude.

• No woman should be forced, coerced, bribed, or paid to kill or sell her children either before or after birth.

• Abortion, whether legal or illegal, poses a danger to a woman's physical, psychological, and spiritual health. Abortion has been linked to breast cancer and increased risk of miscarriage. The easy availability of abortion lowers respect for women, children, and life. Therefore, abortion should be discouraged and governments, families, and communities should address the problems which lead to abortion; namely: sex outside marriage, poverty, and the loss of respect for human life.

• Marriage is the best protection of the rights of the mother. A woman's rights in marriage should be protected. Governments should enact social legislation and tax policies which support marriage. No woman should be forced to marry against her will.

• Male infidelity and promiscuity spread sexually transmitted diseases to chaste wives. All sexual activity outside marriage should be discouraged by law and social pressure.

• The sex industry poses a threat to marriage, to women's reproductive health, to the financial security of families, and to societal respect for women in general. All aspects of the sex industry—prostitution, live sex shows, pornography, explicit films, and videos, including rock videos and advertising which exploits women, should be legally banned and discouraged by social pressure.

• Every mother, in union with the father, should have control over the education of her children.

• Women should receive education which recognizes the diversity of work inside and outside the home which they may perform during their lifetimes. Women's education should recognize the special work of women as educators of their own children.

• Mothers should have time to educate their own children within the home, particularly in matters of religion, family traditions, and cultural heritage. Formal education should not be so demanding on the time or draining of the energy of the children that their family life suffers or that family-centered education is impossible. Public schools should recognize that parents are the primary educators of their children and that the schools are servants of the parents.

- Parents should have the right and economic ability to choose the education they deem most appropriate for their children, including religious education and single-sex education.

- Women should have the right and opportunity to engage in social activism, particularly in those areas where they perceive a threat to themselves, their children, or their families, including the threat of sexual exploitation of children and anti-family media. Freedom of speech and the press shall not be a defense for violations of the rights of parents to protect their children from what the parents determine are pernicious influence or dangers to their children's religious upbringing, innocence, or health.

A real partnership between men and women doesn't require statistically equal housework and employment. Full-time motherhood gives women freedom to control their time and energy, which working mothers often don't have. The division of labor in the family is efficient. Husbands, free from everyday household concerns, can devote their energies to their careers. Well-organized women can manage the housework and childcare, even of large families, and still have time and energy to make an additional impact on society. Women want the freedom to decide what is best for them.

Many women want to be home, but have been forced into the workplace. What women are often not aware of is that the economic pressure on women comes not from inexorable market forces. Someone has planned this, orchestrated it, and is pleased that women are being forced into the workforce. The gender feminists say, "Today women have to work." What they don't say is that they have been working to make sure that every woman has to work.

Thirteen

Council of Europe

Returning home after the PrepCom, some of the pro-family NGOs and delegates had an opportunity to read through the stacks of material they had picked up off the tables around the meeting rooms. Among these was a report from a conference organized by the Council of Europe. This report, entitled "Equality and Democracy: Utopia or Challenge?", shows the link between feminist theory and government programs.

The Council of Europe, which promotes discussions of social and cultural issues among European nations, organized a high-level meeting in the Palais de l'Europe in Strasbourg, 9-11 February 1995, as part of the preparatory process for the Beijing conference. About 250 people attended the meeting, including representatives of the member states of the Council of Europe, other European states, representatives of international governmental and nongovernmental organizations, and experts. The prime minister of Slovenia, Janez Drnovšek, and the deputy prime minister of Sweden, Mona Sahlin, co-chaired the conference. The president of Ireland, Mary Robinson, gave the keynote address. The president of Iceland, Vigdís Finnbogadóttir, presented the final conclusions.

The thirty-nine-page report published in English and French provides an important link between feminist theory and the Gender Agenda of the Beijing platform. Some of the sections of the Beijing platform are open to multiple interpretations, but the Council of Europe report reveals the thinking of those who support the gender perspective and their ultimate goals. The Council of Europe report also reveals that the promoters of Gender Agenda have considerable power and influence, and intend to use it.

In her speech at the conclusion of the meeting, President Finnbogadóttir emphasized the importance of "mainstreaming a gender perspective":

> If we are genuinely convinced of the need to deepen democracy in a structural way, multi-faceted strategies are required so as to cast aside dominant patterns which tend to confine women and men to stereotyped roles in society and we must mainstream a gender perspective in policy-making. [Council of Europe, "Equality and Democracy: Utopia or Challenge?" (Palais de l'Europe, Strasbourg, February 1995), p. 35]

Quotas or Parity

In her speech, President Finnbogadóttir admits that the goal of the woman's movement has changed from *de jure* equality (legal equality), which she admits has been largely achieved to *de facto* equality (statistical equality). In the report it is clear that the participants in Strasbourg clearly understand the obstacles to *de facto* equality and the measures needed to assure that men and woman participate in equal numbers in the various activities of society.

The participants in Strasbourg take it for granted that parity democracy (fifty/fifty, male/female representation) is the goal. The following quote, printed as it appears in the original, is the conclusion of the chapter on the "Equal Participation of Individuals and Groups: The Challenge of Parity Democracy" [Council of Europe, p. 9]:

> In conclusion, many delegations agreed on:
>
> the fact that many women suffer serious inequality where the right to participate in democracy is concerned;
>
> the need to abolish the obstacles which hinder *a priori* such participation (namely, cultural and religious conditioning, social and economic dependence, segregated

education, and training which fails to meet the needs of women);

the adoption, as a means for the active pursuit of equality and towards achieving more representative democracy for all citizens—both men and women—of:

either quotas

or parity.

The report offers various explanations for why equality of opportunity has not resulted in statistical equality:

The group reviewed the various factors explaining the low level of female participation in public life. Among these, particular stress was laid on the issue of maternity (freedom of choice and child care) and differences in the social conditioning of women. [Council of Europe, p. 10]

According to this view, women are forced into motherhood because they don't have access to abortion and child care and because they have been brainwashed into wanting to be mothers. Freedom from motherhood becomes a necessary condition for women's equality. The report takes it for granted that women should choose to run for political office rather than to be mothers. The participants in Strasbourg want to be sure that the next generation of women will be properly conditioned: "Education is an important strategy to change the gender bias in the process of socialisation of boys and girls. Stress was laid on the use of textbooks without the stereotype images of women's and men's traditional roles" [Council of Europe, p. 23].

The stereotypical images referred to are images of women as wives and mothers: "It is high time to make it clear that gender stereotypes are outdated: men are no longer only macho bread-winners and women not only wives and mothers. The negative psychological influence of showing stereotypes of women should not be underestimated" [Council of Europe, p. 26].

The participants in the discussions in Strasbourg appear afraid that merely seeing pictures of women as happy wives and

mothers could tempt women and girls away from political aspirations. The work of the home is viewed as a burden from
which women must be freed so they can achieve parity in political and public life.

"Women must be relieved of the burden of having two
jobs, which can adversely affect their career prospects, disrupt
their private and family life and prevents them from taking part
in political and public life" [Council of Europe, p. 38].

There are no references to women who would prefer to be
relieved of the burden of work outside the home, so that they
could devote their energies to the care of their families.

In the countries in question all women have the legal and
equal right with men to participate in the political process—the
right to vote, to participate in political parties, to run for office,
to lobby. The "inequalities" targeted are not inequalities in the
right to participate, but inequalities in the rate of participation.
Although the participants in Strasbourg do not admit it, what
is really targeted here is women's choices—the choice to be
mothers, the choice not to run for office, the choice to vote for
men rather than women. "Quotas or parity" is the means by
which the advocates of the gender perspective overrule the
decisions of women.

Fundamentals

The Council report makes it clear that equality, defined as
parity, is the standard by which everything else must be evalu-
ated: "The advancement of the equality of women and the full
enjoyment by women of their human rights is a fundamental
legal and moral obligation of the Council of Europe and the
international community" [Council of Europe, p. 16].

The participants in Strasbourg recognized that a strategy
to achieve their version of equality requires "measures designed
to change attitudes" [Council of Europe, p. 11]. And, they
targeted culture, tradition, customary practices, and particularly, religion, as the sources of resistance: "The rise of *all* forms
of religious fundamentalism was seen as posing a particular
threat to the enjoyment by women of their human rights and

to the full participation of women in decision-making at all levels of society" [Council of Europe, p. 13].

One of the problems with dealing with this kind of attack on religion is that religion is lumped with culture and cultural norms. For the secularist all three are human creations and therefore accountable to civil society. There are, of course, real abuses of the equality, rights and dignity of women which have been justified by appeals to culture, to tradition, and even to religion, but freedom of religion is also an important value that must be protected. The report calls for governments to inter-fere with the interpretation of religion: "[G]overnments, reli-gious institutions, and all sectors of society should recognise the legitimate claims of women to have a significant role in the definition and interpretation of religious, cultural and custom-ary norms and should take active steps to encourage women's involvement in these processes" [Council of Europe, p. 18].

In other words, doctrines considered by believers to be God's revealed truth are to be judged and accepted as legiti-mate only if they promote statistically equal participation. Furthermore, the report calls for the Council of Europe to investigate religion: "The Council of Europe should initiate comparative studies into the influences that different cultures, religions and traditions play in enhancing and impeding the full realisation of women's human rights within the member States of the Council of Europe" [Council of Europe, p. 18].

Freedom of religion would, as a result of these policies, be subordinated to the demand for statistical equality.

Sexual Agenda

The reason for the attack on religion is not hard to dis-cover. At the Cairo conference on population, Catholic and Moslem delegates blocked attempts to create new sexual and reproductive rights. Since achieving consensus in this area ap-pears unlikely, the participants reject the consensus system: "While consensus may be a desirable method of proceeding in many circumstances, it was felt that the pursuit of consensus at any cost was potentially dangerous for the full realisation of women's human rights" [Council of Europe, p. 14].

The participants in Strasbourg wanted the expansion of human rights to include the right to abortion, sexual activity outside marriage, adolescent sexuality, and lesbianism:

> The right to *free choice* in matters of reproduction and lifestyle was considered a fundamental right for women. The enjoyment of sexual and reproductive rights is a prerequisite for women to have genuine self-determination. . . .
>
> The voices of young women should be heard since sexual life is not solely attached to married life. This leads to the point of the right to be different, whether in terms of lifestyle—the choice to live in a family or to live alone, with or without children—or sexual preferences. The reproductive rights of lesbian women should be recognised. [Council of Europe, p. 25]

The "reproductive rights of lesbian women" would include the right to adopt children and to utilize sperm banks and other forms of reproductive technologies, including surrogate mothering.

The report blames male control of religion for the failure to achieve "free choice in reproduction": "It is overwhelmingly men who control the process of interpreting and defining the relevant religious, cultural or traditional practices, and as a consequence these norms are defined in patriarchal ways which limit women's human rights, especially in asserting control over women's sexuality and in confining women in roles that reinforce and perpetuate their subordination" [Council of Europe, p. 15].

While this analysis reflects feminist thinking on religion, it ignores the facts. Christian, Jewish, and Moslem teaching condemns all sexual activity outside of marriage—men's as well as women's—and, following the logic of the report, this would limit men's "human rights" as much as it would women's. The traditional religious teachings on marriage, if followed, protect women from sexual exploitation and single parenthood.

The concerns of the delegates to the PrepCom that "gender perspective" concealed advocacy for homosexuality were well founded. What they failed to recognize was that promo-

tion of the gender perspective is invariably accompanied by an
unrelenting attack on traditional religions.

Since the participants at the Council of Europe meeting
included representatives from the governments in the European Union, the report provided a clear indication of what
could be expected from the EU during the Beijing conference.

Part III

Fourteen

The Nondefinition of Gender

When the extended PrepCom ended in April, the draft was still heavily bracketed, and the key word *gender* had not been defined. A contact group was scheduled to meet on 15 May to discuss a definition. The break gave the Gender Establishment time to pressure the poor profamily countries not to accept the profamily definition of gender as referring to two sexes.

The Coalition for Women and the Family tried to influence the delegates to the contact group, with flyers and information about the radical feminist agenda, such as the one shown below:

GENDER
DEFINE IT OR DO NOT USE IT

The word "Gender" has become politicized. If it is going to be used in the text, it must be defined so everyone can agree on what is meant.

Some Radical feminists use "Gender" in contrast to "sex."
"Sex" means the biological reality of male and female.
"Gender" means the social conditioning and cultural practices associated with masculinity and femininity.

Those who push this definition do so because they believe that all the obvious differences between men and women are not natural, but caused by "oppressive gender socialization" and women will be free only when they are no longer forced by their cultures to be feminine.

They further believe that whereas "sex" is fixed, people can choose their "gender." This interpretation is particularly popular among homosexuals and lesbians.

This definition declares war on femininity and natural womanhood.

The "gender perspective" is essentially a Neo-Marxist interpretation of world history, under which "gender," not class or race is viewed as the fundamental category of repression, because gender transcends all categories.

Under the "Gender Perspective" everything is viewed as part of the power struggle between men and women. The "Gender Perspective" in this context means a "sex-class revolution" of women against men.

Before the nations of the world give their consent to any Platform for Action which includes the word "Gender" they should demand a clear definition of the term or replace the term "Gender" with unambiguous language.

Coalition for Women and the Family

Profamily flyers and lobbying proved no match for the behind-the-scenes arm-twisting carried on by the U.S., European powers, U.N. agencies, and other interested parties. An African government official remarked that he had never experienced such pressure. To countries facing severe economic realities, taking a position which would put at risk their relationship with powerful aid donors and those who approve loan applications wasn't an option.

Profamily delegates, mainly from the developing nations, wanted a definition that would include references to two sexes. Their concerns were practical rather than philosophical. They wanted to be sure there was no hidden acceptance of homosexuality in the definition. The EU, Canada, and other advocates of the Gender Agenda wanted a definition which referred to socially constructed roles. The U.S. representative had told the press that the U.S. was hoping for "creative fuzziness."

At the first meeting, the debate immediately bogged down. The delegates from Honduras, Guatemala, Benin, Malta, and the Holy See had all expressed concern about the definition of gender as socially constructed roles. Mercedes Wilson, the delegate from Guatemala, made a passionate plea for a definition of gender which specifically mentioned two sexes and did not include any reference to "socially constructed, determined or ascribed roles." She suggested that the words *sex, male* and *female, feminine* and *woman* could be substituted for *gender* following the pattern of the French translation.

The chairman, Mrs. Selma Ashipala of Namibia decided to take upon herself the task of writing a definition, which was presented at the next meeting. Her definition read as follows:

> During the last Preparatory committee meeting for the Fourth World Conference on Women, an issue arose concerning the meaning of the word *gender* in the conference's draft Platform for Action. In order to examine this matter, the Preparatory committee decided to form a contact group in New York, with the Conference's Rapporteur, Mrs. Selma Ashipala of Namibia, as Chair. The Preparatory Committee mandated the Contact Group to seek agreement on the commonly understood meaning of *gender* in the context of the Platform for Action and to report directly to the Conference in Beijing.

> Having considered the issue thoroughly the Contact Group noted that: 1) the word *gender* has been commonly used and understood in its ordinary, generally accepted usage in numerous other UN fora and conferences; 2) there was no indication that any new meaning or connotation of the term, different from accepted prior usage is intended in the draft Platform for Action; 3) in the context of the Platform for Action the commonly understood meaning of the word *gender* refers to the socially constructed roles played and expected of men and women in society, as well as the responsibilities and opportunities of men and women arising from these roles.

> Accordingly, the Contact Group agreed to reaffirm that the word *gender* as used in the Platform for Action of

the Fourth World Conference on Women is intended
to be interpreted and understood as it is in ordinary,
generally accepted usage. The Contact Group also agreed
that this report be read by the Chair of the Conference
as a Chairperson's Statement and that the statement
should form part of the documentation of the final report of the Conference.

The strange thing about this statement is that it did not
reflect facts. The statement claims that "the word *gender* has
been commonly used and understood in its ordinary, generally
accepted usage in numerous other UN fora and conferences."

For the majority of the delegates participating in these
conferences, English is not their first language, and, therefore,
they rely on dictionary definitions. Searching a number of dictionaries, one finds that the first and primary definition of
gender refers to grammar and describes words. Nouns, pronouns, and adjectives in some languages have a gender, usually
masculine, feminine or neuter. Gender in grammar refers to
classes or groups of things. The secondary definition is as an
equivalent to sex, meaning masculine or feminine. "Socially
constructed roles" that can change was not listed in any English or foreign-language dictionary as a definition.

The definition of *gender* as "socially constructed roles that
can be changed" was not "its ordinary, generally accepted usage." The usage might be generally accepted among feminists,
but they are hardly ordinary. Bella Abzug, in her speech to the
delegates on the subject, had admitted that "the meaning of the
word *gender* has evolved." In fact, a totally new meaning had
been created.

The second statement, "There is no indication that any
new meaning or connotation of the term, different from accepted prior usage, is intended in the draft Platform for Action," also did not reflect the facts. A substantial difference
existed between the way *gender* was used in the Beijing draft
and its use at other conferences.

There is no evidence that this change in the meaning of
gender had been discussed or agreed to by delegates in the

general assembly or in any of the major conferences. The Gender Establishment had simply pushed it through and were clearly determined to protect what amounted to a coup.

The definition offered in the third section of the statement, "*gender* refers to the socially constructed roles played and expected of men and women in society, as well as the responsibilities and opportunities of men and women arising from these roles," represented a total capitulation to gender feminist ideology. Some progender delegates tried to argue that this only referred to situations where women were arbitrarily denied employment, for example as airline pilots. This contention was contradicted by the text of the platform, where the use of the word *gender* appears in almost every paragraph. The insistence on the necessity of "mainstreaming a gender perspective" in every program, and the references to "gender analysis," "gender sensitivity training," "gender issues," "gender aspects," etc., made it clear that what was at stake was much more than whether or not women can be airline pilots.

The impasse was resolved in a way comprehensible only to those accustomed to the Byzantine world of U.N. diplomacy. The delegates at the contact group, over the vigorous objections of Sra. Wilson, deleted the third section and accepted the rest of the statement. Thus, gender is now defined "as it has been commonly used and understood," but no definition is given. Since the contact group was formed because there was no common understanding, this was, to say the least, disingenuous.

It is true that the profamily delegates were not forced to accept a definition that included "socially constructed roles." On the other hand, the promoters of the gender perspective were not forced to admit that there are only two sexes. The nondefinition allowed the U.N. bureaucracy to proceed with their project of imposing a gender perspective on the world and to define *gender* as socially constructed roles.

The promoters of the Gender Agenda considered the nondefinition a victory because they had already inserted the concept of socially constructed gender roles into the Beijing document in two paragraphs. Paragraph 50 [48] refers to "the rigidity of socially ascribed gender roles." Paragraph 28 [27] reads in part:

> The boundaries of the gender division of labour between productive and reproductive roles are gradually being crossed as women have started to enter formerly male-dominated areas of work and men have started to accept greater responsibility for domestic tasks, including child care. However, changes in women's roles have been greater and much more rapid than changes in men's roles. In many countries, the differences between women's and men's achievements and activities are still not recognized as the consequences of socially constructed gender roles rather than immutable biological differences.

It is clear in this context that the reproductive role involving "responsibility for domestic tasks, including child care" under discussion is motherhood.

Later, a number of delegates remarked that they did not understand how this paragraph could have been accepted at the PrepCom. Given the chaos of the debates and the number of contentious issues during the PrepCom, it is, however, not surprising that a great deal of nonsense slipped by the overstressed profamily delegates. Some believe that the size and complexity of the draft were part of a carefully planned strategy. The profamily forces had scored an unexpected victory in Cairo. Their opposition was determined not to be taken unprepared again. With so many controversial sections in the draft—many of which were bound to be controversial—the promoters of the Gender Agenda could be relatively confident that the profamily alliance would concentrate on the sexual and reproductive health sections, and be unable to mount effective opposition to the other aspects of the Gender Agenda.

Denying the Differences

The last sentence of paragraph 28 [27], which says, "In many countries, the differences between women's and men's achievements and activities are still not recognized as the consequences of socially constructed gender roles rather than im-

mutable biological differences," is the heart of the Gender
Agenda. It is also demonstrably false.

Many, although not all, of the differences between men's
and women's activities and achievements are caused by immutable biological differences. Men run faster, are physically stronger, are better at higher mathematics and chess, are more ag-
gressive, and don't become pregnant or nurse. Ample evidence
exists to prove that men's brains, bodies, and hormone levels
differ from women's. Delegates from Third World countries
regarded the mere suggestion that there were no differences
between men and women as absurd.

The Gender Agenda begins with a false premise—the
differences between men and women are social constructs—
and then goes on to demand that this premise be "mainstreamed"
in every program and policy. According to the "gender perspective," since all the differences between men's and women's
activities and achievements are artificial, they can and should
be eliminated.

While the profamily advocates rejected the idea that all the
differences between men and women are social constructions,
they did not embrace the opposite point of view, namely that
all the social and cultural differences between men and women
are caused by immutable biological differences and, therefore,
unchangeable. Most believed that many factors, including biology, the experience of living as a man or woman, culture,
tradition, and free will decisions work together to create the
differences between men and women.

Society, it is true, transmits certain expectations to children, but these expectations are hardly arbitrary, nor can they
be arbitrarily removed and other expectations substituted for
them. Little girls will grow up into women who can become
pregnant. Little boys will grow up into men who are, in general, physically stronger. Encouraging little girls to want to
excel in activities requiring upper body strength or little boys to
want to be pregnant and nurse children would be foolish, and,
therefore, societies have not done it. Associating infant care
with women can hardly be considered arbitrary when the cry of
the newborn causes the mother's milk to be released.

Societies have always divided the labor of the family between men and women. Women have been assigned work which
allows them to be with the children. It would be impractical to
transfer this care to the fathers when the babies have stopped
nursing. It would be far wiser to assign to men the tasks which
require prolonged absence from the home, and, in fact, that is
what most societies have done. This division of labor between
men and women in the family affects the work of men and
women outside the family. While not all men and women
become parents, the majority will and should be prepared to
fulfill those responsibilities.

Educating young people to believe that men and women
are the same, or that motherhood is the same as fatherhood, is
lying to children. The children will soon find out that they
have been deceived. Like the woman who complained to me
that she had been brought up to believe that men and women
were the same, but was now married and had a baby and
realized she had been lied to, today's children will not be pleased
when they grow up and realize that they have been deceived
about such an important issue.

The profamily position supports what can best be described
as "integral complementary," affirming that men and women
are completely equal in humanity, dignity and rights, but different and complementary by nature. Any sexual chauvinism,
either male or female, is absolutely rejected. Neither sex has a
right to claim superiority. Integral complementary is a rejection
of the idea that the biological differences between men and
women are irrelevant or obstacles to be overcome and that men
and women should therefore be treated the same or be the
same. Also rejected is a fractional view of complementarity in
which human traits are divided between men and women in a
stereotyped manner. Integral complementarity insists on the
complete humanity of each person. Man and woman are viewed
not as opposites, but rather, like two eyes which are separated
by a few centimeters giving the human person depth perception. The human race exists only as male and female, and the
differences between the sexes give humanity a depth and insight that it would otherwise lack.

The profamily position is not a rigid defense of the past, but a reasoned attempt to remove those things which artificially restrict women, while protecting women's right to be different. Profamily advocates were willing to enter into debate about what was artificial and what was natural, but the feminists were not open to debate on the subject. For gender feminists, different is unequal, unequal is unjust.

Whatever real injustices may have been inflicted upon women in the past, they will not be rectified by denying women's specific originality or unique feminine nature. Ignoring the differences between the sexes or, worse, seeing them as obstacles, declares war on human nature—woman's nature as well as man's.

Fifteen

Preparations

The gender confusion extended to the Division on Translation and Editing of the U.N., which in May issued a provisional version of its Glossary on Women's Issues—Spanish/English. The glossary translated *gender* as *sexo*, even though Spanish has an equivalent word *género*. The glossary defined *gender/sexo* as

> 1. The sex of assignment by oneself or those who raise the individual. 2. in mod, (esp. feminist) use, a euphemism of the sex of a human being, often intended to emphasize the social and cultural, as opposed to the biological distinctions between the sexes.

This makes no sense. If gender is the equivalent of sex, then it isn't assigned to the person either by himself or his parents. According to this definition, a person's gender could differ from his sex. The glossary went on to define *gender role* as

> The sex of a child assigned by a parent; when opposite to the child's anatomical sex (e.g. due to genital ambiguity at birth or to the parents' strong wish for a child of the opposite sex), the basis is set for postpubertal dysfunctions.

This definition has absolutely no relation to the text or to common usage.

International Coordinator of Associations, Beijing '95

In June a number of profamily women met in Rome to plan for the Beijing conference. Among them were Fenny Tatad, wife of a prominent Philippine senator, Silvia Arcardi from Argentina, and Maria Luisa Lopez from Spain, as well as women from the United States, Latin America, Italy, France, and Germany. They were all concerned about the current form of the draft. The women from Latin America insisted that it was not enough to oppose the current draft. They needed to show their governments and the women in their countries what they were for. They needed an alternative platform.

Although the time was short, these women agreed to put together an alternative platform and circulate it among various groups for input. This effort would have been impossible without a remarkable initiative begun by Ana Garijo of Spain. Before the PrepCom, Sra. Garijo had gathered the signatures of Spanish groups representing thousands of women who opposed the Gender Agenda as it was manifested in the Beijing platform. During the PrepCom, Garijo and her Spanish associates recognized that an international effort was needed. To meet this challenge they organized the International Coordinator of Associations, Beijing '95.

A petition drive on an international scale would have been impossible. They had no way to count and store millions of signatures. Therefore, the coordinator focused on getting support from profamily organizations around the world. The Coordinator distributed a form which listed various points in the current draft and the profamily positions on this issues. Organizations who opposed the draft platform and supported the profamily positions were asked to sign their organization's name, have the form notarized, and sent to Spain. By the time the Beijing conference began, the Coordinator had received signed affirmations from organizations representing over fifty million women.

The signers of the Coordinator affirmed their support for
1) The Universal Declaration of Human Rights which is based on "recognition of the inherent dignity and equal and

inalienable rights of all members of the human family" and includes the "right to life," the protection of the family as "the natural and fundamental group unit of society," the protection of motherhood, the rights of parents to choose the kind of education that shall be given to their children, and freedom of religion.

2) Protection of children and adolescents from invasive, indiscriminate and premature exposure to explicit sexual information.

3) Respect for the work of women within the home and women who choose to be homemakers. *Gender* is a polite way of saying *sex* and refers to two sexes, male and female.

4) Free access for young women to pursue a balanced education to prepare them for life.

5) Condemnation of: all prostitution as demeaning to women; forced birth control and sterilization; pressure to procure abortion; feticide and infanticide as violence against women; and condemnation of the manipulation of the truth concerning health risks of contraceptives and abortion.

6) The right to vote, run for political office, and participate in the political process without discrimination or prejudice.

These positive prowoman positions were contrasted with the draft platform which, according to the Coordinator, promoted "sexual and reproductive rights" including the right to abortion and sexual activity outside marriage for everyone, including adolescents and lesbians; adolescent sex education that promotes unmarried sexual activity and the dispensing of contraception without parental approval; the gender perspective, which is based "on the assumption that motherhood, family, and heterosexuality aren't natural"; non-traditional careers for women over a well-rounded education; voluntary prostitution; and quotas.

The Coordinator agreed to accept responsibility for producing, circulating, translating, and promoting the alternative Platform for Action. With only a little more than two months until the beginning of the Beijing conference, those working on the alternative platform did not have time for all the consultation they would have liked. Still, the version of A Platform for the Women of World contained input from Moslem, Catholic, Baptist, and Evangelical women around the world. The results, although still considered a work in progress, were translated into English, Spanish, Portuguese, German, and French.

The alternative platform began with a section which applied relevant sections of U.N. Universal Declaration of Human Rights to the current problems of women and rejected ideas that "equality" requires statistically equal participation:

> Women and men are different and it is entirely appropriate to recognize those differences, particularly in the family and in regard to motherhood, so long as that recognition in no way disadvantages or discriminates against women. To deny the differences would violate the freedom of women to express and fulfill their unique vocations within the family and society. [A Platform for the Women of the World, A.2]

While the Beijing document mentioned marriage only negatively, and never used the words *husband* or *wife*, the alternative platform reminded people that the Universal Declaration of Human Rights supported the right of all men and women "to marry and found a family."

The alternative platform laid down principles which should govern the implementation of any plan to improve the condition of women. These were, in order of their importance: dignity, equality, complementarity, liberty, responsibility, subsidiarity, solidarity, and realism.

There had been debate during the PrepCom over the word *dignity*. The profamily delegates were astonished that there was opposition to inclusion of a word enshrined in the U.N.'s own Universal Declaration of Human Rights. It appears that the gender feminists were so dogmatic that they were afraid that the word might be interpreted to imply that there was an outside power which conferred dignity on human beings, that they opposed any references to women's dignity.

Those preparing the alternate platform believed that the principle of subsidiarity offered the best way to address women's lack of control over their lives. Subsidiarity requires that larger group units of society not usurp the functions which can be managed and controlled by the small group units, in particular, "the family should have freedom to manage and control its own affairs."

The alternate platform stressed that when power is concentrated in the hands of a few persons, these persons are more likely to be men than women, and women suffer disproportionately from a loss of influence and control. Increasing the number of women in the top levels of government, however, will not compensate for the loss of freedom ordinary women experience in their daily lives. The application of this principle of subsidiarity was seen as a way to "naturally increase the power and influence of women."

The alternate platform promoted the principle of solidarity as an antidote to the class struggle promoted by the Gender Agenda. Solidarity calls on men and women, all classes, races, and groups, to work together and consider the needs and interests of others.

"A Platform for the Women of the World" offered simple concrete suggestions to improve the conditions of women in the areas of poverty, education, health, peace, development, work, the media, the girl-child, and human rights. While the members of the team felt that they might have been able to do better if they had more time, they were pleased that they were able to set down in less than 30 pages—what the Beijing draft could not do in over 150—a plan that really reflected the aspirations of the women of the world.

The Vatican

Pope John Paul II had taken an active role in drawing attention to the Cairo conference, but the stance of the church toward the Beijing conference was very different. The Vatican delegation to the Cairo conference had been under the leadership of the Pontifical Council on the Family, whereas the Beijing Conference on Women came under the Pontifical Council on Laity. In Cairo, the battle lines were clearly drawn. The Catholic church unequivocally opposed abortion, artificial contraception, and sexual relations outside marriage, and supported the family, parental rights, and chastity. The Cairo conference had been under the control of International Planned Parenthood. The Catholic church had no intention of standing by while IPPF imposed abortion on demand on the whole world. At Beijing, while abortion continued to remain a concern, the issue was women.

While feminists portray the Catholic church as antiwoman because of its opposition to abortion and refusal to ordain women, the present pope has repeatedly insisted that the church supports women's equal dignity and rights and opposes all violence and injustice against women. Pope John Paul II had, in his pontificate, written repeatedly on women and used the Beijing conference as an opportunity to reiterate the same themes. On 1 January he issued a letter entitled "Women: Teachers of Peace" in which he wrote, "Authentic peace is only possible if the dignity of the human person is promoted at every level of society." Women, he continued, are called to "become teachers of peace with their whole being and in all their actions" because "to them God entrusts the human being in a special way." The text stressed the complementarity of men and women, motherhood, and the important role of women in the world, and condemned discrimination against women.

In May, the pope received the secretary general of the Beijing conference, Gertrude Mongella, and issued a special letter expressing the Vatican's appreciation of her efforts. John Paul stressed that the conference proposals must be based on "recognition of the inherent, inalienable dignity of women, and the importance of women's presence and participation in all aspects of social life" and "universal human rights." He also pointed out that "equality of dignity does not mean 'sameness with men.' " He warned that "a great sensitivity is required in order to avoid the risk of prescribing action which will be far removed from the real-life needs and aspirations of women."

In June the pope wrote a special letter to women. He also devoted several of his noontime talks to the subject. His attempts to strike a conciliatory note and stress the importance of women's presence in the life of their communities surprised some, who had been convinced that the Catholic church was irredeemably antiwoman. Some commentators even suggested that the pope had changed Catholic teaching in these areas, which was not the case.

If the Vatican had hoped that conciliatory words from the Holy Father or the fact that Mongella was Catholic would influence the progress of the conference, they were disappointed. Mongella's first loyalty proved to be to her friends in WEDO. Near the end of the conference she said, "We are seeing a revolution in the making. . . . I have not been applying my Catholicism to this conference, otherwise it would have been a disaster."

Bella Abzug tried to use the positive statements made by John Paul II to undermine the profamily opposition to certain sections of the platform, implying that the Vatican supported the entire document: "The Beijing Platform for Action is a consensus document agreed to by nations of the world, including the Vatican" ["Bella Abzug defends the Beijing Conference," *The Earth Times* (22 July 1995), INTERNET: theearthtime@igc.apc.org].

At the same time she condemned any criticism of the proposed platform as an attempt to block "efforts to improve the lives of women everywhere and rollback women's gains."

John Paul II stressed the positive. Dr. Joaquin Navarro-Valls, director of the Holy See Press Office, however, expressed concern about ideological imbalance and linguistic ambiguities, noting that gender appeared around two hundred times and mother/motherhood fewer than ten. He questioned the attempt to introduce the term *sexual orientation*, which could refer to pedophilia. In his briefing in August, Navarro-Valls called on the conference to "boldly assume a perspective decidedly in favor of women" and expressed concern that there might be an attempt to impose upon developing countries "a Western product, a socially reductive philosophy, which does not even represent the hopes and needs of the majority of Western women."

The Lancet

In July, an editorial in the prestigious British medical journal *The Lancet* reviewed the proposed Beijing platform's section on health and found it lacking:

> Health is defined in a surprisingly one-dimensional manner; it seems to exist in a reproductive context only. When seen through the lens of fertility control, the notion of "health" is distorted beyond all recognition. This intellectual astigmatism leads the UN—and influential non-governmental organizations such as the International Planned Parenthood Federation—to adopt empowerment and equality as cure alls. . . .

> Halfdan Mahler, Secretary General of IPPF, characterises those who oppose his organisation's agenda—one that is largely identical to that of the UN—as "obscurantist opposition." . . . One does not have to be either "conservative" or "extremist" to use Mahler's words, to question the assumptions on which the reproductive health and family planning "movement" is based.

> Politically correct slogans draw easy support and much needed funds. They sting public apathy and indifference. But they should be examined carefully and critically before they become the basis for policy. The new colonialism of the international women's health agenda is a dangerous strategy. It places western utopianism before local pragmatism, expert notions of what is right before a culturally specific understanding of need. Equality means far more than achieving the right to reproductive health. ["Women in the World," *The Lancet* (22 July 1995), p. 195]

Public Debate

In Cairo the profamily forces had been organized by Catholic and prolife groups. After Cairo many Evangelical Protestant Christians realized that they needed to be involved. In particular, Beverly LaHaye, of Concerned Women for America, and Dr. James Dobson, of Focus on the Family, took an active part in the preparations for Beijing.

From his base in Colorado, Dr. Dobson's radio shows and literature reach an audience of millions around the world with a profamily message. In August he sent an eight-page letter to his supporters condemning the U.N. conference as "the most radical atheistic, anti-family crusade in the history of the world." Dobson expressed outrage over the holding of a conference on women in China, a country notorious for violations of the human rights of women. He cited China's forced abortion and forced sterilization policies, the continued practice of female infanticide and female feticide, the scheduling of executions of prisoners in order to harvest and sell their organs, and the eating of aborted human fetuses. He also condemned the Clinton administration for refusing to grant political asylum to Chinese women fleeing China's one-child policies.

Dobson pulled no punches, condeming the use of U.S. resources and power to "undermine the family, promote abortion, teach immoral behavior to teenagers, incite anger and competition between men and women, advocate lesbian and homosexual behavior and vilify those with sincere religious faith."

He pointed to the gender feminist ideology as the cause of the problem and encouraged his supporters to "derail this gender feminist juggernaut." Besides the letter he devoted several radio shows to the topic and made several speeches against the conference.

The members of the U.S. delegation reacted swiftly, insisting that the document was profamily. President Clinton insisted the conference was "true blue to families" ["Transcript of 26 August Remarks by President, First Lady on the 75th Anniversary of Ratification of the 19th Amendment," *U.S. Newswire*, 28 August 1995]. Profamily spokesmen tried to inform the public about the contents of the draft, and they were primed for a public debate over the Gender Agenda. Instead, feminists and administration spokesmen denied the radical contents of the draft, feigned ignorance of the Gender Agenda, and talked about how the conference would promote the health and safety of women. Members of the U.S. delegation waved a small kit containing the supplies needed for nonhospital maternity care, insisting that this was what Beijing was about and dismissed the gender controversy as irrelevant.

President Clinton had promised that his appointed delegates would be diverse and bipartisan; however, as has been typical of the Clinton administration, no one associated with the profamily movement or prolife movement was on the delegation.

Former Congresswoman Marjorie Margolies-Mezvinsky, deputy head of the U.S. team in Beijing during a roundtable discussion televised on C-Span, denied accusations that the conference was promoting an antifamily agenda: "I would never take part in anything that didn't celebrate the family. . . . I've adopted children when I was single, came into marriage with my husband's children . . . so I wouldn't be considered the 'traditional family.'" She did allow however that "this document is not telling people about what is right." When asked about whether or not the U.S. would protest the Chinese treatment of women, she replied, "We will try not to be judgmental."

Profamily spokespersons found it difficult to get their message across in the thirty-second sound bites allotted to them. It was difficult to explain that the document was flawed because of what was not in it. The defenders of the conference quoted the positive sections of the draft, trying to leave the impression that opponents of the draft opposed these when, in fact, there was no opposition to positive prowoman programs.

The profamily forces did, however, reach sympathetic members of Congress with their concerns. The new Republican (and profamily) majority was eager to take on the administration. Profamily Republican Congressman Chris Smith had attended the Cairo conference, where he had been forbidden to speak publicly. The 1994 election gave the profamily members new power to hold hearings and ask tough questions. On 7 March during hearings before the House International Relations Committee, Congressman Smith questioned Secretary of State Warren Christopher. Smith asked why, when she was asked to identify the U.S. delegation's prime concern in Beijing, the first thing delegate Margolies-Mezvinsky said was "choice" and when asked to specify what choice, her response was "abortion" [Hearing of House International Relations Committee, 30 March 1995].

Aware that during the Cairo conference, the State Department had sent a memo to ambassadors ordering them to put pressure on foreign governments to support the U.S.'s position on abortion, Smith demanded assurances from the secretary that the administration would not use the conference to try to change the laws of other countries regarding abortion.

The Chilean Statement

The debate over the Beijing conference went on in many countries, with varying results. From the profamily point of view the most positive action came from the Chilean Senate, which issued a strong statement expressing concern about "any totalitarian value system that claims to have the authority to represent the conscience of the men and women of our world." The statement summarized the profamily position on the issues raised in the platform:

> Types of families—We want to endorse the concept of the family, fundamentally the monogamous and stable union of a man and a woman in matrimony, as the basic cell of society. Any type of action that would have the effect of weakening the family should not be endorsed; the earth trembles at the possibility that persons of the same sex constitute family. All this, of course, must be done, without prejudice, to protect the persons and especially the women, children, and dependent persons. To be precise, it is necessary to consider in justice the problem that other kinds of unions present, whose members and children merit protection.
>
> Gender Equity—Because many proponents of the use of the word *gender*, without great specificity, maintain that masculine and feminine refers only to cultural and social construction and not to the biological conditions which mark the psychological make-up of the woman and the man, and that according to this conception the differences between the sexes do not have a natural origin, considering the consequences that this unleashes for

all the individuals as well as for the family and society, we are repelled by the pretentious circumlocutions and troubled by what we believe is a use of ambiguous terms and legal concepts that emanate from them.

Equality of Opportunity—We believe that the Chilean position should clearly recognize the equality of opportunity which ought to exist between men and women. We desire, furthermore, that the different roles of the father and the mother in a complementary manner within the family be recognized. We hope that maternity will be valued, together with the family and work within the home.

Reproductive rights of women—This wording, which appears to us to be highly troublesome and dangerous, is frequently used to imply the existence of a right to abortion, the so-called reproductive freedom. We want a clear and definitive definition which defends of the right to life of all human beings from the moment of conception without any type of ambiguity or liberal semantic interpretations. We desire that Chile as expression of its culture would veto any phrase or action that could be understood directly or indirectly as legitimizing abortion.

The rights of parents in the education of their children: The Senate demands that no action be approved which violates the rights, duties and responsibilities of parents and other persons legally responsible for children, and also in all actions that affect them as adolescents, in conformity with the Convention on the Rights of the Child.

In general, we do not want a presentation that is not founded on a pretended inferiority of the woman, but a declaration which respects the liberty and dignity of women as persons and as active agents in the construction of society and if it is her will, also as wife and mother in the family. [author's translation]

In the U.S. the debate over the content of the draft was sidetracked by the controversy over the jailing of human rights activist Harry Wu. Many voices were raised against Hillary

Clinton's attendance at a conference in China while Harry Wu remained in jail under threat of execution. Others felt that China's human rights violations were so atrocious that the U.S. should boycott the conference entirely.

In August, the U.S. State Department issued a warning to U.S. citizens attending the conferences, "that delegates could face arrest and imprisonment if they carried Bibles into China, engaged in religious activities or met in small groups."

A number of groups decided to boycott the conference to protest Chinese policy. The Independent Women's Forum, which opposes feminist extremism, chose not to go, but provided articulate women to debate the issue in the media and distributed buttons which read "SEX IS BETTER THAN GENDER."

In addition, the problems over accreditation were not resolved until the end of July. Only then did a number of U.S. NGOs know if they would be allowed to send representatives. To make matters worse, the representatives found they couldn't make room reservations without a visa, and they couldn't get a visa without an NGO accreditation.

Washington Times reporter George Archibald kept the issue in the news, and local talk shows took an interest, but the major media ignored the real story and followed the administration line. Unfortunately some of the best profamily legislators and commentators were distracted by the five genders debate and disappointed when they discovered that the document did not actually mention five genders.

On 1 August the U.S. Senate approved an amendment to the Foreign Relations Revitalization Act instructing the U.S. Delegation to Beijing that "motherhood" must be "recognized as a valuable and worthwhile endeavor that should in no way . . . be demeaned by society, or by the state." Sen. Kay Bailey Hutchinson of Texas who introduced the amendment said that this resolution "puts Congress on the record that the U.S. delegates should advocate the importance of the family as the fundamental unit of our society. . . . Most Americans would be surprised to learn that there is any reason for Congress to take this step."

Senator Coats, in a speech during the debate said that the current Beijing draft "conflicts with the views of most Americans and is silent on the unique role of women as mothers."

This resolution and a similar move from the House of Representatives had an effect on delegates from other countries, but it was not sufficient to stop the gender juggernaut which was rolling toward Beijing.

As the end of August approached, the pseudoissues were resolved. Harry Wu was tried, convicted, and exiled in time for Hillary to attend the conference. Controversy over the site of the NGO forum, which had been moved from Beijing to a third-rate town forty minutes from the conference, had been intense. There had even been talk of moving the conference to another country. Some of the profamily delegates had prayed it would be canceled completely. But, in the end, the U.N. capitulated entirely to the Chinese government.

Members of Non-Governmental Organizations who had struggled for months to receive accreditation from the U.N. found they had to face another barrier. The Chinese refused or delayed granting visas—no reasons were given. Dorothy Patterson, from the Southern Baptist Convention, had visited China several times in the past, but in spite of a number of appeals was denied a visa. Dan Zeidler, a key organizer of the Coalition for Women and the Family, had to travel from his home in Wisconsin to Chicago several times before he finally wheedled a visa out of the Chinese officials. The Chinese strategy appeared to be stall and delay and then give in only to the extremely persistent.

Sixteen

China

Huairou

The grubby industrial city of Huairou, chosen by the Chinese to host the Non-Governmental Organizations Forum, lacked even the charm of poverty. The Chinese had used the pretext that the facilities in Beijing were structurally unsound and couldn't accommodate the thirty thousand anticipated participants, but everyone knew that they simply did not want thirty thousand feminist activists let loose in their capital city. The U.N. had protested the change of venue, but, as with everything else, in the end, everyone kowtowed to the Chinese. The NGO forum began a few days before the actual conference.

The Chinese authorities regarded the entire assembly with suspicion and were rumored to be especially concerned about lesbian activists. They evidently had seen the C-Span coverage of a feminist rally in Washington, D.C., where feminists had demonstrated bare-breasted and, therefore, supplied the police in Huairou with blankets to protect the populace from any visually shocking displays.

The Chinese authorities made it plain that free speech and protests in support of dissident ethnic groups, particularly the Tibetans, would not be tolerated. Participants unaccustomed to real oppression complained about the rough treatment by the Chinese police. Those who hoped that holding the conference in China would be a step toward greater freedom for Chinese women found their optimism unwarranted. There was no opportunity for dialogue with ordinary women.

The Chinese did allow five thousand carefully selected and trained women party members to attend the forum. These served as another arm of the authorities. When the Ecumenical Coalition on Women and Society tried to draw attention to the lack of religious freedom in China, a Chinese woman grabbed their petitions for religious liberty and dashed out of the meeting tent ["The Lack of Liberty—An object lesson," *Faith & Freedom* (Winter 1995-96), p. 10].

Although the Chinese officials had promised everything would be ready on time, when the women arrived in Huairou, they found unconnected telephones and showers that didn't work. The accommodations were poor to awful. Huairou, at its best, has little to recommend it; heavy rain and wind turned it into a giant puddle. The tents set up for regional, theme, and diversity meetings flapped wildly in the September winds, providing little protection from the cold and rain. The school buildings, where the workshops were held, were dreary and cold on the rainy days, unbearably stuffy on the sunny.

Hillary Clinton was supposed to speak at an outdoor parade group, but a driving rain forced the drenched participants into a dingy converted movie theater which held only fifteen hundred. Founding feminist Betty Friedan was shoved around by the police trying to control the crowd and then left outside among those stranded in the rain ["Women fight past Chinese security at forum," *Providence Journal* (7 September 1995), p. 10a].

Workshops

The forum events included over three thousand workshops, on such topics as "Lesbian flirting," "Guided Meditation for the Healing of Mother Earth," "Celebrate the Goddess," "Lesbianism for the curious," "Lesbian activism from an interfaith perspective," "Women in black: a gathering of spirits" (participants were instructed to wear black and bring a lamp), "Lesbian and mother" (artificial insemination), and "How religious fundamentalism helps the spread of AIDS."

Danish and Swedish sex educators presented a workshop on their programs to a standing-room-only crowd. Women were standing around the edges of the room and sitting on the floor as one of the teachers explained with great enthusiasm how she teaches adolescents "lust and desire are a resource in people's lives" that youth should make use of. There were no references to marriage or even love. The Danish sex educator admitted that there are laws against sex with children under fifteen, but saw nothing wrong with two fourteen-year-olds having sex with one another. Audience members from the U.S. complained that repressive attitudes and the Religious Right prevent the adoption of such "progressive" programs in their country.

The sex educators distributed a booklet entitled "Sexual Rights of Young Women in Denmark and Sweden," which credited compulsory sexual education programs for the progress made in modernizing the sexual attitudes. According to the booklet, younger Nordic women now have among other things:

- a secularized childhood

- a high sexual self-esteem

- a relatively early sexual debut

- frequent intercourse-rate

- orgasm

- pluralistic sexual technique

- [written or visual] . . . sex materials. ["Sexual Rights of Young Women in Denmark and Sweden" (The Danish Family Planning Association and the Swedish Association for Sex Education, RFSU, 1995) p. 8]

Young women's sexual rights in Denmark and Sweden include the right to:

- choose a sexual partner

- control over one's body

- sexual pleasure

- safe abortion

• knowledge in general and of services and rights. ["Sexual Rights," p. 9]

In Danish compulsory sex education courses adolescents are "acquainted with their rights and protection under law— including their sexual and reproductive rights." Parents who protested to the European Commission on Human Rights that compulsory sex education was a violation of their religious beliefs were informed that "compulsory sex education does not per se infringe on the freedom of religion."

The authors of the booklet appear pleased that, as a result of these programs, "many children are born out of wedlock without causing any kind of stigma. . . . Marriage has to some degree been replaced by consensual unions" ["Sexual Rights," p. 14].

Forum Activities

WEDO sponsored a series of daily meetings entitled "Daughters of the Earth," which included various forms of goddess worship. A Brazilian participant declared, "The people in my community used to believe in the crucifixion, but we have decided, 'No more crucifixion.' We believe in life. . . . We are power."

The overflow crowd responded enthusiastically. Bella Abzug led them in a passionate chant, "I am power! I am power!" ["Goddesses of Their Own Choosing," *Faith and Freedom* (The Institute on Religion and Democracy, Winter 1995-96), p. 7].

The World Council of Churches sponsored a seminar entitled "Gospel, Cultures and Women" at which the speaker denounced traditional Christianity as imperialistic, patriarchal, colonialist, capitalistic, egocentric, racist, and homophobic. Presbyterian church (U.S.A.) staffer Rebecca Peters, blamed "messages from the Bible, from church tradition and authorities" for "domestic violence, incest, child abuse, and sexual exploitation of girls and women by clergy" ["Church Delegates Join Attack on Faith," *Faith and Freedom*, p. 8].

Ecumenical Women United, an international umbrella organization which includes World Council of Churches, the

World Wide Lutheran Church, World Federation of Methodist Women, the World Alliance of Reformed Churches, among others, organized a workshop entitled "Religion: between Fundamentalism and Self-awareness." The first speaker discussed the need to break away from tradition. "We are worried about fundamentalism, since the traditional religions are a hindrance to the growing-together of the world." A Scandinavian Lutheran leader called for radical changes. "We must invent new ceremonies. Everybody should evolve her own form of religion." The participants applauded enthusiastically.

While feminists greatly outnumbered them, the profamily groups also set up booths in Huairou and held workshops. The booth set up by Susan Roylance of United Families promoting motherhood and family was extremely popular. One woman was so pleased to find a profamily presence in the sea of feminism that she burst into tears.

Several of the profamily workshops were disrupted by feminist protesters, who accused the speakers of wanting "to control women's sexual lives." Lesbians tried to distract the profamily speakers by lying in each other's arms and fondling each other provocatively during the sessions.

A group of Moslem women bought a bulletin board and decorated it with prolife and profamily posters. When a group of lesbians tried to tear it down, one of the women's sons defended the women and the board from their attack. However, the next morning they found it smashed to pieces.

When the Moslem women held a small demonstration singing, "Man and woman hand in hand, makes our world a happy land," a group of lesbians harassed and taunted them. The lesbians kissed and hugged one another, laughing at the Moslem women, trying to pull off their scarves and kiss them.

Claiming to speak for all the women at the forum, the WEDO-controlled Linkage Caucus put forward a list of the changes they wanted in the platform. In particular, the Linkage Caucus demanded the deletion of all profamily references. The profamily women attending the forum were quick to respond with flyers in English, Spanish, and French which read as follows:

N G O ALERT!
WOMEN'S LINKAGE CAUCUS
DOES NOT SPEAK
FOR THE WOMEN OF THE WORLD
AT THE NGO FORUM

Delegates to the Beijing Conference should not be deceived by statements made by the Women's Linkage Caucus and other caucuses controlled by WEDO (Women's Environment and Development Organization) and Bella Abzug. They *do not* represent the sentiments of women around the world.

The WEDO-controlled Women's Linkage Caucus is using the NGO Forum to achieve their own agenda.

WEDO, the Women's Linkage Caucus and Bella Abzug have ignored the real concerns of the women, wives and mothers of the world.

WEDO and the Women's Linkage Caucus think there is nothing wrong with aborting girl babies as long as you don't know they are girls.

WEDO and the Women's Linkage Caucus think 13 year-old girls can negotiate safe sex.

WEDO and the Women's Linkage Caucus oppose "abstinence until marriage as responsible sexual behavior."

WEDO and the Women's Linkage Caucus want every country to be forced to accept homosexual and lesbian rights and behavior.

WEDO and the Women's Linkage Caucus oppose mention of parents (mothers) rights. Don't they know women are parents too?

WEDO and the Women's Linkage Caucus plan to use words like "forced pregnancy," "full respect for physical integrity of the human body," "unsafe abortion," "safe abortion," and "sexual and reproductive rights, including the right to have the information and means to exercise those rights" to deceive countries and to push abortion on demand.

WEDO and the Women's Linkage Caucus oppose the inclusion in the Beijing document of "the dignity" of women, of "religious," "ethical" and "spiritual" values, and of "maternity."

WE PROTEST THIS MISREPRESENTATION

Beijing

Coalition for Women and the Family members warned that the accommodations in Huairou would be primitive and had made reservations in Beijing, traveling to Huairou only when necessary. It proved a wise, but expensive choice. Unfortunately, the hotels assigned to NGO's were a thirty-minute taxi ride from the site, and the buses that were supposed to shuttle participants back and forth from the conference remained parked in front of the hotels. Participants had to negotiate with taxi drivers who couldn't speak English or wait in line for thirty minutes while Chinese police rationed taxi cabs. The Chinese had doubled the prices on everything and were determined to wring every penny possible from the participants.

Luckily, Tom Minery of Focus on the Family discovered the Catic Plaza, a brand new hotel, adjacent to the conference center, which had just been opened and set aside for the press, but, which was, in spite of its convenient location, almost empty. Key members of the Coalition for Women and Family moved to Catic and set up a command center in a tenth-floor suite.

The Catic Plaza looked as though it had been ordered from the U.S. in a kit and assembled in a hurry by workers who didn't know how to use a caulking gun or cut carpet straight. Mao jackets and drab revolutionary styles had been banished. The restaurant hostesses wore full-length pink suits slit up to the thigh, and bowed gracefully. The young women at the reception desk were lovely and smiling in their matching suits, but it was impossible to communicate with them in English, Spanish, or French.

Since most Chinese couldn't speak English, the coalition was particularly fortunate that an American couple who live in a provincial Chinese city had come to Beijing to translate for them. The couple helped the coalition negotiate room rates, and acquire a copy machine and cell phones. When these were added to the computers and printers they had brought with them, they had the technology to conduct a full-scale campaign.

Some coalition members dubbed the Catic "the Catholic Plaza." A Catholic priest from Scotland had tried to say Mass in the religious center set up on the conference grounds, but when he refused to work with the break-away Chinese Patriotic Catholic Church, he was told he would have to leave. So, he moved the twice-daily Masses to a suite in the Catic. The two rooms were frequently so packed with worshipers that there was no place to kneel. A priest from the Philippines also offered daily Mass at the Catic, and there were Evangelical Christian services. The coalition members were worried at first that the Chinese might object to the religious services and the other activities of the coalition or that their rooms or phones might be bugged. However, as the days passed and nothing happened, they stopped worrying.

Beijing was not at all what the participants had expected, probably because Beijing was not at all like Beijing. Those who had visited the city only months before couldn't believe the transformation. Three million transient residents had been shipped out of town. Many Beijing residents had been given a two-week holiday. Buses had been banned from the streets, easing air pollution and allowing the visitors to breathe. Automobile use was restricted. Even the bicycle lanes were relatively empty.

Beijing was uncharacteristically clean. Flowers, previously declared bourgeois extravagances, had been planted around the city. Potted chrysanthemums were massed in the middle of the sidewalks near the complex, and while they were extremely decorative, they forced the pedestrians into the street. Restrictions on vehicle and pedestrian traffic designed to keep Chinese people out of the conference made negotiating around the site difficult, but other than that, the participants in Beijing were not harassed by the Chinese police.

Seventeen

The Fourth World Conference on Women

On the first day, the chairman brought up the question of the definition of *gender*. Profamily delegates were still concerned, but several of the profamily delegates were worried that a definition of gender might be worse than an ambiguous statement. The majority of delegates from profamily nations and the Holy See agreed to accept the nondefinition which had been proposed by the contact group rather than face the possibility of something worse.

Mercedes Wilson, from Guatemala, was not satisfied and asked that gender be defined as "male and female: the two sexes of the human being." No one supported her. Mercedes was devastated. The feminists were ecstatic.

All pretense of seeking consensus was abandoned in Beijing. Discussion in the main committee skipped from section to section, making it difficult for the lobbyist to prepare. Any issue that was not immediately resolved the way the leadership wanted was referred to a contact group. There were no set meeting rooms for contact groups, and the times of the meetings were often changed. Concerned profamily delegates were forced to run upstairs and down trying to find the meetings.

When they arrived, the meeting might be over and the results declared final.

To make things even more difficult, no translation was offered in the contact groups. This clearly disadvantaged the profamily delegates who came mainly from Latin America, French-speaking Africa, and the Moslem countries. Since the debate was over language, correct translation was crucial. Protests about these abuses were ignored.

The bilingual members of the Coalition for Women and the Family volunteered as translators. In this capacity, they were able to advise sympathetic delegates about the implications behind the language. While efforts were made to ban them from the meetings, most persisted.

In the contact groups, there was no attempt to arrive at a true consensus. Majority ruled unless the majority disagreed with the leadership, and then the decision was postponed. Since the composition of the contact groups was, in many cases, a reflection of nothing more than the ability to find the meeting room, a majority of those present should not have been binding on the entire conference. The consensus system had protected the rights of all countries by including nothing in the document that was offensive to any group of nations. The new system forced the will of those running the conference on everyone else.

Most delegates from the Third World regarded the sexual agenda of the Europeans as totally irrelevant to their cultures. For them, men and women are different, motherhood and family are important. They were willing to tolerate what they regarded as European nonsense because they expected to be rewarded with substantial aid to help the women in their countries. Halfway through the conference, however, it became clear that there would be no money for aid. The rich countries let it be known that they expected the poor ones to divert already-scarce resources from health and education to "mainstreaming the gender perspective." After this revelation, the mood turned extremely nasty. One of the African delegates complained, "If there is no money, why are we here?" The coalition used this quote as the headline for a flyer:

"IF THERE IS NO MONEY,
WHY ARE WE HERE?"

Developing nations had been led to believe that if they put up with all the nonsense coming from the EU, they would have money for development.

Now they are told there is no money.

And what is worse, the EU expects the developing countries to use their scarce resources to fund the promotion of its cultural agenda in their own countries.

It will be the same old story, the scarce funds will go to pay "experts" from developed countries, who will tell the people in developing countries how to live their lives.

Poor women can't feed their children the paper they are using for "gender disaggregated statistics."

Developing countries know the impact of illiteracy, polluted water, and poverty on women. They don't need to pay for "gender impact analysis" to tell them that women will benefit from increased spending on development, basic health care and education.

REJECT THE EU's CULTURAL IMPERIALISM
DON'T SACRIFICE YOUR COUNTRY'S
VALUES
FOR NOTHING

Coalition for Women and the Family

The representatives of the European Union blatantly demanded that the document be written their way, stating bluntly what they would accept and what they would not. In the contact groups the group leaders insisted that the participants "make progress," which always meant progress toward accepting the demands of the EU, and "compromise," which meant surrender to the EU.

While the EU claimed to be defenders of women, time and time again the interests of real women were surrendered to ideological considerations. Nothing illustrates this more clearly than the debate over prostitution. The Third World countries wanted the platform to condemn "all forms of prostitution."

The EU insisted that the condemnation be limited to "forced" prostitution and child prostitution. And, the EU prevailed.

According to many sources this outcome was imposed by the Netherlands, with the backing of the Nordic nations. Feminists argue that legalized prostitution protects the "well-being" of prostitutes. While this wording was opposed by the majority of delegates, the chairman did not tell the Netherlands to make a reservation.

The ideological extremism was evident in the section on violence against girls, which condemned "paedophilia, forced prostitution and possibly the sale of their organs and tissues, violence and harmful practices such as female infanticide and prenatal sex selection, incest, female genital mutilation and early marriage, including child marriage" (paragraph 41).

It was difficult to understand why a distinction was made between "forced" and "voluntary" prostitution for girls, when there was none made between "forced" and "voluntary" pedophilia, child marriage, and genital mutilation.

The antiprostitution groups lobbied hard for a forthright condemnation of all prostitution, insisting that the sex trade, particularly in Asia, targets poor women and children and spreads AIDS to innocent wives and babies. They accused the EU of protecting the Asian "scum" that traffics in women. The African nations unanimously demanded that prostitution be condemned as a violation of human rights.

Wassyla Tamzali, of the Coalition against Traffic in Women, regarded the substitution of the words *forced prostitution* for *all forms of prostitution* as a catastrophe and a step backward from the 1949 U.N. Convention for the Suppression of the Traffic in Persons and of the Exploitation of the Prostitution of Others. The convention condemned prostitution and traffic in persons because they are "incompatible with the dignity and worth of the human person and endanger the welfare of the individual, the family and the community." According to Tamzali, "After Beijing, it is going to be necessary to begin again at zero" ["Retour à la case départ," *Vivre*, 13 September 1995, p. 2 (author's translation)].

The lack of true concern for women was also evident in the discussion of paragraph 110(e), which had been proposed by an oncologist from Slovakia. She suggested the following wording: "Inform women about data which show that hormonal contraception, abortion and promiscuity increase risks of developing cancers and infections of the reproductive tract." When this section came up for discussion in the main committee, the Egyptian chairman refused to call on her, although she stood for thirty minutes waving her flag. After the section had been discussed and her wording deleted, she was recognized and complained bitterly, "There is no way you could not see me. I am tall, six months pregnant."

U.N. Agencies

Those concerned with the environment should be asking how many trees have to die to keep the U.N. in nonrecyclable paper. The conference area was literally strewn with booklets and printed matter of all kinds, much of it produced by U.N. agencies. If only the paper, money, and ink used for these materials could have solved the world's literacy problem. In the final days of the conference, I saw a large flatbed truck being loaded with stacks of U.N. materials which had not been distributed. If the U.N. has a financial crisis, cutting off its printing budget would probably go a long way to solving the problem.

The U.N. agencies producing this blizzard of paper had not waited for the Beijing conference to authorize the "mainstreaming of the gender perspective." They had already written it into everything. There were materials on "Gender Issues in Rural Fisheries," "Gender poverty and employment," "Toward a Gender-inclusive Culture through Education," and even "Gender Analysis and Forestry Training." A coalition member who reviewed numerous U.N. publications complained, "These people cannot promote simple projects like literacy or women's health without trying to push contraception and abortion."

In this regard the World Health Organization is the biggest offender, blatantly promoting the legalization of abortion in member nations where it is currently banned. A WHO pamphlet charged that antiabortion laws in the Philippines impinged upon women's "capacity to think and act as independent and rational human beings"; implied that legal abortion was more important to women than employment or education; dismissed postabortion syndrome as an attempt by "anti-abortion activists . . . to shift the debate from moral to scientific grounds"; and called on governments to waive parental permission for "family planning services, including abortion" ["Women's Experience of Abortion in the Western Pacific Region," *Women's Health Series*, vol. 4 (Manila: World Health Organization, Regional Office for the Western Pacific, 1995), pp. 4, 6, 25].

Another WHO publication aggressively promoted "appropriate information, skills and services" (read contraception and legal abortion) for "young people who are sexually active" in the same section as it admitted that girls are frequently pressured by "older people to have sex" [*World Health: The Magazine of the World Health Organization: Executive Summary*, 1995, p. 10]. And, one study "among girls aged eleven to fifteen years found that 40 percent reported the reasons for their first sexual intercourse as 'forced' " [*World Health*, p. 14].

In another section, the publication insisted that earning an income was essential to women's good health. A misguided prescription, since overwork, particularly during pregnancy, is a major health problem for women, as other articles in the magazine clearly pointed out. Women whose husbands support them during pregnancy are at far less risk than women who have to work.

Still another WHO publication went so far as to blame "female malnutrition and anemia" on the "religious institution" that embodies "the concepts of exclusive roles for men and women and the conviction, for instance, that women are incapable of ordination because of their sex" (obviously referring to the Catholic church). According to the author, the church's teaching encourages parents to feed the boys rather than the girls [Rebecca Cook, "International Law and Women's Health," *Gender, Women, and Health in the Americas* (WHO & Pan American Health Organization, 1993), p. 250].

The use of the WHO to promote abortion, teen sex, and attacks on religion undermines respect for the agency. This could have tragic consequences in an age where plagues and diseases fly by jet plane.

U.S. Delegation

The U.S. delegation had opposed the inclusion of positive statements about motherhood, family, and spirituality during the PrepCom. In Beijing they had to face the new political realities back home. They had been warned by both Houses of Congress to support motherhood. Just to make sure they didn't forget, Republican Congressman Chris Smith came to Beijing and met with them.

His intervention had the desired effect. The U.S. delegation retreated to the sidelines while Canada and the European Union took the point position. A French delegate made it clear that the Europeans were eager to lead the charge: "In Cairo we took a back seat; now we advance with knives drawn."

The effect of Congressman Smith's visit could be observed during the negotiations. During one of the small group discussions on the risks of adolescent sexual activity, the question was, "Should the statement speak of the risks of all adolescent sexual activity or only 'unprotected' and/or 'premature' sexual activity?" The profamily nations objected to the word *unprotected* on the grounds that all adolescent sexual activity contains risks for young women. They wanted the word *unprotected* replaced with the word *premature*.

The discussion was so heated at one point, the delegates from the EU said that they would not accept any language which stigmatized teen-age sexual activity. When the Vatican delegate pointed out the physical and psychological risks of early sexual activity, the EU delegate retorted with a comment about married teen-agers. The Vatican delegate replied that they did not encourage teen marriage. The group leader began counting heads trying to force through the word *unprotected*. When the group leader ticked off the people on her side, she included the American delegate among those who supported "unprotected." The American delegate, who had been silent through the discussion, reminded the group leader that the U.S. hadn't stated its position. It was clear that the group who did not want to stigmatize adolescent sexual activity believed the U.S. delegate was on their side and that the U.S. delegate was being very careful about committing herself publicly.

The U.S. delegation also reversed the position it had taken at the PrepCom and supported the two positive paragraphs inserted by the Holy See—30 [29] and 31 [24]. While seen as a great breakthrough, the paragraphs gave only token recognition to motherhood and spirituality. Paragraph 30 does state, "The social significance of maternity, motherhood and the role of parents in the family and in the upbringing of children should be acknowledged."

In the context of the antimotherhood tone of the rest of the document, this was a significant admission, but it was not reflected in the rest of the document. When profamily delegates tried to introduce the phrase "portraying happy families, nurturing mothers with their children" into a section of the media, it was deleted.

The biggest tragedy in Beijing was that the real problems of women were neglected. Fatana Ishaq Gailani, a stunningly beautiful matron from Afghanistan, tried to draw the attention of the delegates to the plight of the women in her country, who suffer as the civil war continues, fueled by outside groups. All she wanted was food for the refugees, education, and medical care. "No one is fighting for peace," she complained. "The eyes of the world are no longer on Afghanistan, but women are widowed, children are fatherless, sons are dying."

NGOs

The U.N. bureaucracy has granted NGOs various forms of access to the process, including the right of selected NGOs to address the plenary session of the conference, but not all NGOs were equally welcome. Dr. Margaret Ogola, a pediatrician in charge of an AIDS hospice in Kenya, was among those waiting to make an application to address the plenary. When the U.N. person in charge saw Dr. Ogola's résumé, she sent everyone else away and then asked Dr. Ogola if she worked for IPPF.

Without waiting for an answer, she went on to say, "I don't want you to get the feeling that I'm interrogating you, but all these extremist pro-life groups who are unbalancing the proceedings, I'm trying to keep out." Dr. Ogola, who did not reveal her prolife connections, was immediately granted permission to speak.

As part of their lobbying effort, the Coalition for Women and the Family held an open meeting. The presentations were in four languages and included women from around the world. Dr. Ogola expressed the disappointment she said was shared by African women that feminists were indifferent to the problems of poor women: "In Africa, people are dying of malaria, pneumonia and other infection but the Beijing platform only mentions abortion, abortion, and yet again abortion. If they really wanted to help African women and if they took the trouble to speak to them, they would understand that abortion is just about the least thing which African women worry about."

Gwen Landolt, of Real Women of Canada, spoke against the inclusion of "sexual orientation" as a protected category and criticized the Canadian government for ignoring the will of the people by trying to force gay rights on the country. During the question and answer section, lesbians took issue with Mrs. Landolt's comments, and the meeting deteriorated into a shouting match.

Seeing China

After a week of nonstop negotiations with little progress on the most controversial issues, the participants took Sunday off to see the sites. Beijing sits in the middle of a great plain. Straight roads lined with trees lead north to the Great Wall. Once outside the city, the single-story brick houses give way to rich fields of corn and orchards heavy with fruit. As one approaches the wall, the mountains rise sharp and angular, like a Chinese painting.

Tienamen Square lay across town from the conference center. On one side of a Communist monument a giant clock ticks off the seconds until Hong Kong becomes Chinese again— a reminder of China's imperial ambitions. Chinese propaganda newspapers prepared for the conference made it clear that China expects to get Taiwan back, and one senses that China's ambitions do not stop there. Those who expect prosperity to be the first step to freedom should study Chinese history and remember that the present rulers of China are first of all Chinese, walking in the tradition of the emperors, and are only tangentially Communist.

Across a wide boulevard from the square stands the rostrum from which the Chinese elite review the troops. In the center of the rostrum, a massive painting of Mao watches over everything. Beneath Mao the great doors are open to the once-forbidden city. The residence of Chinese emperors for five hundred years has opened its outer courts to Sunday strollers and shoppers, its inner sanctum to foreign tourists.

On the balmy Sunday afternoon, family groups out for a walk invariably consisted of a single pudgy child accompanied by four or five adults, reflecting the reality of two generations of China's one-child policy.

China is raising a generation of "little emperors and empresses," spoiled by two protective parents and four doting grandparents.

The scene reminded me of the only real encounter I had with the ordinary people of China. On the plane to Beijing I sat next to an elderly Chinese woman and her son. When I told her that I had three sons and one daughter, she looked at me as though I was the most favored of women.

Eighteen

Parental Rights

To young people encouraged to use "lust and desire as resources," contraception and abortion are necessities and parental consent a major obstacle. Therefore, it was not surprising that the EU should fight against all references to parental rights. The coalition made up a number of flyers to inform delegates of the importance of parental rights:

WHY IS THE E.U. OPPOSED TO PARENTS'
RIGHTS?

E.U. delegates have repeatedly defended sexual relations for unmarried adolescent girls.

The E.U. wants to prevent concerned parents from protecting their daughters from:

> Sex education teachers like the Swedish and Danish sex educators at an NGO Forum workshop in Huairou, who said they promote "lust and desire" to adolescents;

> Women's health clinics who will give girls condoms and abortions without their parents' knowledge;

> Lesbians who will teach them lesbianism is normal and their parents are judgmental.

Why does the E.U. think it knows what is best for Moslem girls, Latin American girls, and African girls?

TELL THE E.U. TO LEAVE OUR
DAUGHTERS ALONE

RESTORE PARENTAL RIGHTS

Coalition for Women and the Family

The Youth Caucus, which was strongly influenced by
WEDO and the Lesbian Caucus, countered with a flyer that
opposed parental rights, which read in part:

EMPOWERMENT OF WOMEN BEGINS
WITH YOUNG WOMEN

Support the rights of the girl child and
young women.

Adolescents have right to information and education
essential for their well-being, as recognized in the Convention on the Rights of the child.

PROTECT WOMEN'S RIGHTS

Parents must respect the evolving capacities of the girl
child and young women in accordance with the Convention on the Rights of the Child.

*Access to education information and services is a health
issue.*

The belief systems of parents must not undermine the
rights of the girl child and young women to sexual health
and reproductive health information and services.

*Delete the repetitive passages overstating the rights,
duties and responsibilities of parents.*

EXAGGERATING PARENTAL RIGHTS DISEMPOWERS
WOMEN

Youth Caucus

The coalition lobbied hard, but it was difficult to convince
delegates from the Third World that their families were at risk.
Many had been convinced that sex education was necessary to
prevent the spread of AIDS. Coalition members pointed out
that these programs have been tried in the U.S. and unwed

pregnancy and sexually transmitted diseases have increased because contraceptives all have established failure rates.

Third World delegates could not understand why the developing countries would be pushing these programs if they were failures. Coalition members explained that the real goal of the programs was to break down moral and religious values and encourage sexual experimentation and activity among children of all ages, and in this they were succeeding.

Olivia Gans of Abortion Victims of America found it effective to ask delegates from Africa to guess how many abortions were done in the U.S. in a year. The delegates would respond that since in America no one was poor and there was sex education and access to contraception, they would guess 200 to 300. They were shocked to discover the number was 1.5 million.

A Sudanese delegate demanded of a French delegate, "Why are you so angry, you have all those rights you want us to accept. . . . Please show me a little window of your paradise, because all I see in your world is increased promiscuity among young people, increased divorce, increased abortion, homosexuality, venereal diseases. . . . I don't see your paradise."

When the contact group on parental rights met, the pro-family contingent, having been tricked in the past, was present in force. As the majority, they agreed to the following wording: "Recognizing the responsibilities, rights and duties of parents and other persons legally responsible for adolescents to provide, in a manner consistent with the evolving capacities of the adolescent and in conformity with the Convention on the Rights of the Child appropriate support and guidance, in sexual and reproductive matters."

Two days later, the chairman from Canada produced copies of a totally different version. Mercedes Wilson protested, "When the western countries have a majority, you just close the case and report it to the main committee. When we, from the developing countries have majority, you want to continue negotiating. What kind of dictatorial process is this?"

The Canadian chairman of the contact group replied that she had discussed the language with several delegates and they had agreed to the change. Mercedes checked with other profamily delegates who had been involved in the original negotiations and all denied that they had been asked about or agreed to the new language. Another contact meeting was scheduled and appeared to be deadlocked, but the chairman waited until Mercedes was forced to leave the meeting to attend a prescheduled press conference where she presented the letter from Mother Teresa to the conference. The Canadian chairman then pushed through the new wording, which read:

> Taking into account the rights of the child to access to information, privacy, confidentiality, respect and informed consent, as well as the responsibilities, rights and duties of parents and legal guardians to provide, in a manner consistent with the evolving capacities of the child, appropriate direction and guidance in the exercise by the child of the rights recognized in the Convention on the Rights of the Child, and in conformity with the Convention on the Elimination of All Forms of Discrimination against Women. In all actions concerning children, the best interests of the child shall be a primary consideration. (paragraph 108e)

This is no longer parental rights language, but children's rights language. If children have the right to privacy and confidentiality, parents have no rights where it really matters. Who decides the best interests of the child? Abortion providers, bureaucrats pushing contraception and abortion, sex educators. Many people had opposed the Convention on the Rights of Child on the grounds that it would be used to subvert parental rights. Here was clear proof that their concerns were justified.

Mercedes expressed her anger at the process:

> We came here to find consensus. How can there be consensus when one side expects the other to sacrifice their religion, their values, their sovereignty? It would have been better if we had divided into two groups. Let all those who want sex for unmarried girls, and explicit sex education and condoms and abortions, single mothers, lesbian marriage, and all women forced to work outside the home stand up on one side. And all those

who stand up for the family based on marriage between a man and woman, motherhood, parental rights, protection of girls from sexual exploitation and the defense of human life from conception on the other. Then we could have had two documents and the people of the world could decide which document really represents the women of their country.

The only bright light in this darkness was Mother Teresa's statement, which the coalition translated into five languages and distributed to the delegates. Mother Teresa spoke directly to the issues being debated:

> I do not understand why some people are saying that women and men are exactly the same, and are denying the beautiful differences between men and women. All God's gifts are good, but they are not all the same. . . . No job, no plans, no possessions, no idea of "freedom" can take the place of love. So anything that destroys God's gift of motherhood destroys His most precious gift to women—the ability to love as a woman. . . . Those who deny the beautiful differences between men and women are not accepting themselves as God has made them. . . . I have often said, abortion is the greatest destroyer of peace in the world today, and those who want to make women and men the same are all in favor of abortion.

Sexual Orientation

Lesbians make up less than 1 percent of the world's women, but they seemed to dominate the lobbying in Beijing. The Lesbian Caucus offered various amendments to the Platform for Action. In addition to calling for "sexual orientation" to be included with race, religion, and other protected categories, their amendments called for a "transformation of society" that would "remove gender hierarchy" and for education programs to "address violence against women including pressures to conform to heterosexual norms." They wanted "family" replaced with "various forms of families." They also wanted the Convention on the Elimination of All Forms of Discrimination Against Women to be amended to "establish freedom of sexual choice for adult women as an inalienable human right."

During the PrepCom the lesbians had won support from various European Union nations and Canada to have the words *sexual orientation* added to four paragraphs of the document. Although the words were bracketed, the advocates of lesbian rights were hopeful that they could prevail. If some delegates had been under the impression that "sexual orientation" referred to a form of sex education, by the time the issue was debated everyone knew that "sexual orientation" meant granted protected status to homosexuals and lesbians.

The lesbians received preferential treatment from the conference organizers. Profamily women who conducted a silent protest at the U.S. press conference had their credentials confiscated and were placed under house arrest. But, when the thirty members of the Lesbian Caucus unfurled a large purple banner reading, "Lesbian rights are human rights," during the plenary session on 8 September, no action was taken against them.

Knowing the issue would be contentious, the leadership delayed the discussion of this issue until the very end. The chairman said that the negotiations would begin at seven o'clock in the evening, but the session did not begin until eleven o'clock. Actual negotiations on "sexual orientation" did not start until two o'clock in the morning.

The Islamic and African delegates were not deterred by these tactics. One of them said, "We know what they are trying to do. They are waiting for us to get so sleepy and tired that we will go home and then they can pass these controversial issues that would be so destructive to our nations. So we are not leaving and we will remain in this chair until they begin, even if we have to stay here all night."

When the negotiations finally began, delegation after delegation rose to demand the removal of the phrase "sexual orientation." The speakers said they had come to Beijing to discuss the problems of hunger and poverty and not to legalize illegality. When, in spite of all the maneuvering, it became clear that there was no way the prolesbian forces could rig a consensus, Chairman Patricia Licuanan, from the Philippines, ruled that since the term had not been aired in the U.N. before, and given the strong opposition, the term should not appear in the text. Canada and the U.S. both requested twice that the language be reconsidered. It was five o'clock in the morning when the meeting ended.

WEDO labeled the opposition to sexual orientation "an historic display of public bigotry." In spite of the overwhelming repudiation of the term by the delegates, WEDO claimed that they had actually won.

> The Platform for Action does not use the words *sexual orientation* anywhere in the 135-page document or declaration. However, most groups consider the pathbreaking Beijing conference debate on the subject of nondiscrimination, based on sexual orientation and the affirmation of human rights of all females, to have been a significant victory for gay and lesbian rights. ["A Brief Analysis of the UN Fourth World Conference on Women Beijing Declaration and Platform for Action," WEDO]

The entire EU and 16 other countries including Canada, South Africa, and the U.S. issued interpretive statements on paragraph 48 [46] noting that they understand that the term *other status* includes discrimination on the grounds of sexual orientation.

A member of the coalition commented as the conference drew to an end that the proceedings were the equivalent of date rape. The EU and its allies, unable to get what they wanted by persuasion, resorted to force, and then claimed they had the consent of their victims.

Reservations

The coalition members harbored a secret wish that at least one country would refuse to join the consensus, but they realized that no diplomat could risk even the appearance of opposing women's rights and equality. Therefore, as the end approached, coalition members began to lobby the delegates to make strong reservations during the final session. The following flyer was distributed in three languages:

WE DO NOT CONSENT

The Platform of Action which will leave the Conference of Beijing is a direct attack on the values, cultures, traditions and religious beliefs of the vast majority of the world's people in both the developing and developed world. While there is much in the Platform that is good and necessary for the advancement of women, the positive portions are overshadowed by the negative. The document doesn't respect human dignity, seeks to destroy the family, totally ignores marriage, minimizes the importance of motherhood, seeks to impose depraved sexual attitudes, promotes homosexuality, lesbianism, sexual promiscuity, and sex for children and seeks to destroy the authority of parents over the children.

We, as citizens of the developed countries wish to apologize to the people from the less developed world and to stand in solidarity with them in defense of family, motherhood, and parental rights. We are ashamed of the way our countries have supported a process of forced "consensus" by denying translation, ignoring delegates from small nations, and stone-walling delegates who objected.

We stand in solidarity with delegates from developing countries who have defended family, motherhood, and parental rights. We promise you that when we return to our countries we will fight to change the policies which are oppressing yours and to let our people know the truth about how you were abused in Beijing.

No objective person looking at this process, where representatives of the rich countries have bludgeoned the delegates from poor countries into submission, could call it consensus.

We wish that the delegates from the less developed world would stand up and say, "No. No, we do not consent to this travesty." But we are realistic. We know how difficult this would be. We know we are asking poor countries to surrender the little they have. Perhaps, somewhere in the world there is one country so poor that there is nothing the rich countries can take away from it, who will have the courage to speak publicly the truth about this Platform for Action.

It is tragic that the developing countries have to hide behind national sovereignty to defend universal principles of respect for the family, motherhood, marriage, morality, and chastity, as though these were peculiar backward customs.

We have seen how they have treated the reservations made in Cairo and other conferences, nevertheless reservations are the only way left to protest these abuses.

If you feel you have no choice but to join the consensus, do not give up your last chance to protest,

PLEASE MAKE STRONG RESERVATIONS
IN THE PLENARY

Member from Developed Countries of the NGO Coalition for Women and the Family.

The delegates from developing countries responded positively to this flyer. Some of them came back and asked for additional copies for their fellow delegates. Others thanked the coalition members for their help. The promoters of the "gender perspective" may have manipulated the process, but they had not won hearts or minds. Profamily participants mourned the fact that an unrepeatable opportunity to address the real problems of women had been wasted.

The platform generated a record number of reservations, as country after country took exception to the antifamily provisions, making hollow any claim that consensus had been achieved. In a moment of unusual candor, the delegate from Malawi expressed the hope that taking reservations would not prevent them from getting funding from the rich nations.

As the conference drew to an end, Gertrude Mongella declared the proceedings a complete success. She reacted defensively when a reporter asked her to respond to charges made by some NGOs that the Platform for Action is antifamily and antimotherhood. "Is education and eradicating illiteracy antimotherhood? Is calling for peace anti-motherhood?" [Li Xing, "Mongella predicts complete success," *World Women*, 14 September 1995, p. 1]. She did not point to sections of the platform which supported full-time mothers or women's work in the home because there were none.

Nineteen

Conclusions

I am often asked to explain what I saw in Cairo and Beijing in a sound bite of thirty seconds. At the risk of oversimplification, I reply that I observed that the U.N. is inhabited by people who believe what the world needs is
1) less people
2) more sexual pleasure
3) the elimination of the differences between men and women
4) no full-time mothers.

These people recognize that increasing sexual pleasure could increase the number of babies and mothers. Therefore, their prescription for world salvation is
1) free contraception and legal abortion;
2) promotion of homosexuality (sex without babies);
3) sex education courses to encourage sexual experimentation among children, and to teach them how to get contraception and abortions, that homosexuality is normal, and that men and women are the same;
4) the elimination of parental rights so that parents cannot prevent children from having sex, sex education, contraception or abortions;
5) fifty/fifty, male/female quotas;
6) all women in the workforce;
7) discrediting all religions that oppose this agenda.

This is the "gender perspective," and they want it "mainstreamed" in every program at every level in every country. For those who look at the world from this gender perspective, the Beijing conference was a tremendous success. They have convinced themselves that in Beijing they won a mandate to impose their Gender Agenda on every family in the world.

They are not foolish enough, however, to believe that they can sell this agenda to ordinary people. Therefore, the Gender Agenda is packaged in rhetoric about equality and rights and talk of families, health, and fairness. They talk about improving the lives of women, but it is women who are being attacked—women who want to be at home with their children, women who want to protect their children from sexual exploitation, women who want to work in "traditional" jobs, women who don't want radical feminists and lesbian activists claiming to speak for them, women who believe that God is their loving Father in heaven.

The Future

I am sometimes asked if I think the Gender Agenda will succeed. It is certainly possible, given its momentum and the power of the Gender Establishment. Universities, educational establishment, government bureaucracies, the media, and big businesses are already falling in line.

The Gender Establishment, no matter how hard they try, however, will not be able to change human nature. Men and women will continue to be different. Women will find ways to mother, but the Gender Agenda, if implemented, would undermine the family and society and increase unwed pregnancy and divorce. The children raised in the ensuing chaos would become dependent on governments whose resources are already strained, emotional and economic debtors draining the accounts built up by their fathers and mortgaging their futures. If the sexual liberation promoted by the Gender Agenda is not checked, sexually transmitted diseases and sexual addictions will spread throughout the world. And, when these things happen, the Gender Establishment would undoubtedly view the havoc their policies caused and see only justification for more funding, more control, and more "gender sensitivity training." But, no matter how much control they have, no utopian sex/gender classless society will ever appear.

However, there is another possibility. If the Gender Agenda is pushed too far, what may appear is a nasty, brutish backlash against not the excesses of the Gender Agenda, but women's rights and equality. The farther the pendulum swings in one direction, the farther it will swing back in the other. Men may decide they have had enough and start acting like the oppressors the feminists accuse them of being. If a real war between the sexes breaks out, women will be forced to choose between militant feminists and the men in their lives. My bet is most of them will choose the men. In such a war, the casualties may be the real gains women have made in the last hundred years.

This generation of feminists, although they would be loath to acknowledge it, have benefited from the good will of a generation of men raised to respect their mothers and, by extension, all women. Feminism would never have won so easily if men had not been trained to be polite. The next generation of women may not be so fortunate. They may have to face hordes of unmothered, father-deprived men who will be far less sympathetic to women's concerns. Teachers are already remarking on young men's sullen resentment to "gender sensitivity." The violent rap music coming out of the welfare ghettos, which glorifies rape and uses the most vulgar terms to refer to women, reflects a world where fatherlessness is a way of life.

Exposure

What can be done to stop the Gender Agenda? The first step is obviously exposure. Gender feminists have left a paper trail, and they must be made to eat their words. Gender feminists who hide behind family language need to be exposed. A perfect example of this kind of deception is Hillary Clinton's book, *It Takes a Village*, which is full of wonderful, apparently profamily wisdom. Underneath, however, one finds the gender feminist ideology. The book should be titled *It Takes a Federal Bureaucracy* because the village Mrs. Clinton envisions isn't a close-knit community where neighbors share common values and support one another, but a place where families are dependent on government programs.

Mrs. Clinton may pay lip service to stay-at-home moms, but she pushes "government subsidized day care." And, underneath the homey little stories, there is a pure gender feminist, who writes: "It may be that women will achieve economic and social parity with men only when mothers and fathers fully share responsibility for rearing their children and other household tasks" [Hillary Clinton, *It Takes a Village* (New York: Simon and Schuster, 1996), p. 212].

Gender feminists cannot be allowed to pretend to be for the family and motherhood, while at the same time they tear down everything that supports the woman in her home.

The more that ordinary people know about the gender perspective, the less they like it. But, it is not enough to condemn their seven-point plan—to rail against sex education, abortion, and homosexuality—or to promote motherhood and family. If one accepts their diagnosis of the problem, then their solutions can appear plausible.

The opponents of the Gender Agenda must attack their diagnosis:

1) The population explosion is about to become a birth dearth. Honest demographers know that failing birth rates, particularly in developed countries, and increased longevity are about to create an economic disaster of monumental proportions, as an aging and infirm population is forced to rely on a shrinking group of workers. History shows rather conclusively that in underdeveloped countries, economic development is triggered and supported by dramatic population increases. Falling population triggers economic collapse.

2) The people promoting sexual pleasure do not understand what sex is all about. They are promoting an infantile, immature, self-centered pleasure-seeking that can never fulfill the longings of the human heart. In the same issue of *Gloria* Steinem's *Ms.* magazine that carried a glowing report on the Beijing conference, there was an article entitled "Sexual Pleasure Unscripted," which quoted, among others, Debra Haffner of SIECUS. Without going into the graphic details, the point

of the article was that feminism has freed women sexually so that intercourse is no longer as important, and masturbation is viewed as "a natural, completely rewarding route to sexual pleasure."

In Gender Agenda's view of sexuality, there is nothing wrong with bisexual transsexual Kate Bornestein promoting a world of polymorphous perversity. This is not liberation, but sickness. Kate Bornestein isn't a hero of the revolution but a tragic figure—a man who had his genitals amputated and dresses up like a woman and then says he's a lesbian. These people need therapy, not followers.

The supposedly sexually liberated become addicted to sterile sensations, always seeking ways to increase the thrill because what they do can never satisfy the human person who has been made for the private pleasures of a faithful marriage and the joys of children.

What is most reprehensible about the sexual liberationists is that they are targeting children, hoping to addict the innocent to solitary sexual activities and exposing them to sexual predators and dangerous behaviors. We have turned our children over to sex molesters and exhibitionists masquerading as sex educators. What is needed is a sexual counter-revolution, not to diminish the pleasures of human love, but to free people from self-destructive, addictive behaviors.

3) Men and women are different. Trying to teach children they are not will not work, as the following article, written by an eighth-grade student demonstrates. Ricky Beyer's class was sent to a "Gender Conference," where, according to Ricky, "the conference leaders were trying to indoctrinate the students," telling them that "each and every human was equally male and female."

> Our neuterist indoctrinator further opened our minds to the fact that "males" and "females," as society names them, are the same. We were told that individuals have no morals, ideas, instincts, or minds of their own beyond what is implanted there by society. When we argued that "men" and "women" had different instincts beyond what society implanted in them, we were treated

with incredulity, and the neuterist indoctrinator did not
even deign to answer our argument. Ignoring us, he
instead called on a "girl" who said, "This is the 90's.
Human's don't have instincts!" [Ricky Beyer, "Indoctrination: Gender Rules" *The Blue and the Gray* (Baltimore
MD: Gilman School) February 1995, p. 1]

Adults should not lie to children. Statistical equality is not
a noble goal, but a totalitarian scheme to shift power, not to
ordinary women, but the feminist elite who would become the
tyrants of the new world order.

4) Women have a right to mother—women have in a
special way been entrusted with the human person. No woman
should be forced, pressured, coerced or in any way deprived of
her right to have children and to care for her own children.

Celebrating women's motherhood in no way diminishes
the many other activities and pursuits of women, nor does it
slight the accomplishments of women who are not biological
mothers, but denying women's right to mother diminishes every
woman.

I consider myself very fortunate that I was able to be at
home with my children while they were growing up. I have
seen the pain in the faces of young women who are forced to
work and leave their babies with others, and I have seen the
economic sacrifices that other women have made to be at home
with their children. If wisdom is knowing the difference between what must be accepted and what can be changed, then
the wisdom for today must be that the present situation does
not have to be accepted. Every woman should have the right to
decide for herself if she wants to make motherhood her primary vocation and to have the opportunity to care for her
children for as long as she thinks is necessary—not as long as
an employer or the government gives her leave.

It will take more than exposure and brilliant arguments. If
this is a culture war, then it must be fought with culture as well
as arguments. The warriors should be writing stories, singing
songs, and creating images that communicate the truth about
the human person.

And, it will take calculated rudeness. The feminists have relied on the politeness of men. They have demanded that dangerous nonsense and utter stupidity be treated with respect. The Gender Agenda cannot be defeated until people are willing to stand up and say, "No more inclusive language, no more politically correct speech." We must refuse to say "gender" when we mean "sex." Those who are offended by reality and human nature will just have to live with it.

Women around the world have been standing up and saying loud and clear, "These feminists don't speak for us." Local, national, and international groups of grassroots women have organized to fight various aspects of the Gender Agenda. I met many of these women in Beijing and know that each one of them represented thousands more at home.

The Gender Agenda reminds me of a giant balloon in a small room. So long as everyone treats the balloon with respect, it continues to expand, and, eventually, it will suffocate the people in the room. But, all that is needed to stop the balloon is one sharp pin. This book is intended to be that pin.

We welcome comments from our readers. Feel free to write to us at the following address:

Editorial Department
Vital Issues Press
P.O. Box 53788
Lafayette, LA 70505

More Good Books from
Vital Issues Press . . .

The First Lady:
A Comprehensive View of
Hillary Rodham Clinton
by Peter & Timothy Flaherty

Is Hillary Rodham Clinton a modern career woman or an
out-of-control feminist? In this compelling account of her
life, the authors suggest that Mrs. Clinton has been misrep-
resented in the media and misunderstood by both
conservatives and liberals alike.

ISBN 1-56384-119-3

ADD:
. . . the facts . . . the fables
. . . hope for your family
by Theresa Lamson

ADD (Attention Deficit Disorder) is often ridiculed by
those cynics who deny its existence and by those who
dogmatically insist that "spanking your child more" would
correct all of his behavior problems. However, if you're the
parent of a child who suffers this disorder, you are painfully
aware that ADD is real. Cheer up! You're not a bad parent.
You need hope, encouragement, and biblical solutions—
this book offers you all three. In addition, the author shares
valuable knowledge from the secular pool of current information.

ISBN 1-56384-121-5

How to Be a Great Husband
by Tobias Jungreis

In marriage, failure is *not* an option. This user-friendly, upbeat guidebook gives men easy, practical suggestions on how to keep their marriages vibrant for a lifetime. Unique features include insightful lists of do's and don'ts and dozens of ideas drawn from a myriad of real-life situations. *How to Be a Great Husband* offers a refreshing approach to the "work" that is marriage, giving husbands invaluable insight on how to achieve success in this most important area of their lives—insight they can apply at the dinner table tonight! Read this book and discover how easy it is to be a "ten" among men.

ISBN 1-56384-120-7

Handouts and Pickpockets: Our Government Gone Berserk
by William P. Hoar

In his new book, William P. Hoar, a noted political analyst, echoes the sentiments of millions of Americans who are tired of being victimized by their own government. Hoar documents attacks on tradition in areas as diverse as the family and the military and exposes wasteful and oppressive tax programs. This chronicle of our government's pitiful decline into an overgrown Nanny State is shocking, but more shocking is Hoar's finding that this degeneration was no accident.

ISBN 1-56384-102-9

Legacy Builders:
Dad, What Does Your Life
Say to Your Wife and Children?

by Jim Burton

Today, feminism and changing economics make it difficult for men to understand their role in a society that seems to devalue their inherent qualities. Discover how men can build a legacy—and why America so desperately needs men to understand their role in the family and society.

ISBN 1-56384-117-7

Dark Cures:
Have Doctors Lost Their Ethics?

by Paul deParrie

Those who trust doctors to look out for the health and well-being of patients need to know the facts about modern medicine. Paul deParrie documents the shift in medicine from traditional ethics to paganism and morbid social engineering and exposes the consequences of this unwise move. From value assessments of patients' lives, to the harvesting of organs from living people, to the use of aborted babies in the production of cosmetics, this book exposes the side of medicine those in the field don't like to talk about. Anyone having any contact with the modern health care system, however, cannot afford to ignore the vile facts.

ISBN 1-56384-099-5

Beyond Political Correctness:
Are There Limits to This Lunacy?
by David Thibodaux, Ph.D.

Author of the best-selling *Political Correctness: The Cloning of the American Mind,* Dr. David Thibodaux now presents his long awaited sequel—*Beyond Political Correctness: Are There Limits to This Lunacy?* The politically correct movement has now moved beyond college campuses. The movement has succeeded in turning the educational system of this country into a system of indoctrination. Its effect on education was predictable: steadily declining scores on every conceivable test which measures student performance and increasing numbers of college freshmen who know a great deal about condoms, homosexuality, and abortion, but whose basic skills in language, math, and science are alarmingly deficient.

ISBN 1-56384-066-9

Children No More:
How We Lost a Generation
by Brenda Scott

Child abuse, school yard crime, gangland murders, popular lyrics laced with death motifs, twisted couplings posing as love on MTV and daytime soap operas (both accessible by latch-key children), loving parents portrayed as the enemy, condom pushers, drug apologists, philandering leaders . . . is it any wonder that heroes and role models are passé? The author grieves the loss of a generation but savors a hope that the next can be saved.

ISBN 1-56384-083-9

Combat Ready
How to Fight the Culture War
by Lynn Stanley

The culture war between traditional values and secular humanism is escalating. At stake are our children. The schools, the liberal media, and even the government, through Outcome-Based Education, are indoctrinating our children with moral relativism, instead of moral principles. *Combat Ready* offers sound advice about how parents can protect their children and restore our culture to its biblical foundation.

ISBN 1-56384-074-X

Out of Control—
Who's Watching Our Child
Protection Agencies?
by Brenda Scott

This book of horror stories is true. The deplorable and unauthorized might of Child Protection Services is capable of reaching into and destroying any home in America. No matter how innocent and happy your family may be, you are one accusation away from disaster. Social workers are allowed to violate constitutional rights and often become judge, jury, and executioner. Every year, it is estimated that over 1 million people are falsely accused of child abuse in this country. You could be next, says author and speaker Brenda Scott.

ISBN 1-56384-080-4

Conquering the Culture:
The Fight for Our Children's Souls
by David Paul Eich

Remember Uncle Screwtape? He was the charming C.S. Lewis character who tried to educate his nephew, Wormwood, on the art of destroying souls. Now, from a fictional town in Montana, comes a similar allegory. This compelling book is a valuable source of support for parents who need both answers and courage to raise moral children in an immoral world.

ISBN 1-56384-101-0

Getting Out:
An Escape Manual for Abused Women
by Kathy L. Cawthon

Each year, four million women are physically assaulted by men who claim to love them. Of these millions of women, nearly 4,000 die. Kathy Cawthon, herself a former victim of abuse, uses her own experience and the expertise of law enforcement personnel to guide the reader through the process of escaping an abusive relationship. *Getting Out* also shows readers how they can become whole and healthy individuals instead of victims, giving them hope for a better life in the future.

ISBN 1-56384-093-6

In His Majesty's Service:
Christians in Politics
by Robert A. Peterson

In His Majesty's Service is more than a book about politics. It's a look at how real men have worked out their Christian beliefs in the rough-and-tumble world of high-level government, war, and nation-building. From these fascinating portraits of great Western leaders of the past, we can discover how to deal with some of the most pressing problems we face today. This exciting, but historically accurate, volume is as entertaining as it is enlightening.

ISBN 1-56384-100-2

Do Angels Really Exist?
Separating Fact from Fantasy
by Dr. David O. Dykes

Have you ever seen an angel? Don't be too quick to answer "no." For most of us, angels evoke images of winged, white figures frolicking from one cloud to another. But, according to the Bible, angels are God's armored warriors ready to protect His kingdom in heaven, as well as His beloved followers on earth. By citing dozens of fascinating angel encounters, the author presents evidence that angels roam the earth today, protecting and comforting God's people. You might be encountering angels without even knowing it.

ISBN 1-56384-105-3

The Best of HUMAN EVENTS:
Fifty Years of Conservative Thought and Action
Edited by James C. Roberts

Before Ronald Reagan, before Barry Goldwater, since the closing days of World War II, HUMAN EVENTS stood against the prevailing winds of the liberal political Zeitgeist. HUMAN EVENTS has published the best of three generations of conservative writers—academics, journalists, philosophers, politicians: Frank Chodorov and Richard Weaver, Henry Hazlitt and Hans Sennholz, William F. Buckley and M. Stanton Evans, Jack Kemp and Dan Quayle. A representative sample of their work, marking fifty years of American political and social history, is collected here in a single volume.

ISBN 1-56384-018-9

The Blame Game:
Why Society Persecutes Christians
by Lynn Stanley

The liberal media is increasing its efforts to suppress Christian values and religious freedom. At the same time, liberal courts and organizations such as the NEA are working to eliminate religion from American culture. In *The Blame Game,* Lynn Stanley exposes the groups attacking the constitutional rights of Americans to tradition and freedom of religion. Also, she explains what these factions fear from mainstream America and why they seek to destroy it through their un-American system of wretched moral relativism.

ISBN 1-56384-090-1

Outcome-Based Education:
The State's Assault
on Our Children's Values
by Peg Luksik & Pamela Hobbs Hoffecker

From the enforcement of tolerance to the eradication of moral absolutes, Goals 2000 enjoins a vast array of bureaucratic entities under the seemly innocuous umbrella of education. Unfortunately, traditional education is nowhere to be found in this controversial, strings-attached program. In this articulate and thoroughly documented work, Luksik and Hoffecker reveal the tactics of those in the modern educational system who are attempting to police the thoughts of our children.

ISBN 1-56384-025-1

High on Adventure:
Stories of Good, Clean,
Spine-tingling Fun
by Stephen L. Arrington

In the first volume of this exciting series of adventure stories, you'll meet a seventeen-and-a-half-foot Great White shark face-to-face, dive from an airplane toward the earth's surface at 140 M.P.H., and explore a sunken battle cruiser from World War II in the dark depths of the South Pacific Ocean. Author and adventurer Stephen Arrington tells many exciting tales from his life as a navy frogman and chief diver for The Cousteau Society, lacing each story with his Christian belief and outlook that life is an adventure waiting to be had.

ISBN 1-56384-082-0

High on Adventure II:
Dreams Becoming Reality
by Stephen L. Arrington

Join the former Cousteau diver again as he travels around the world, revisiting old acquaintances from the deep and participating in dangerous, new adventures. In this exciting second volume of the series, Arrington even explores the underwater lava flow of an active volcano—while it is in progress!

ISBN 1-56384-115-0